MICHAEL

SCHARF

FOR

KID

ROCK

TOTAL

FREEDOM

SPECTACULAR BOOKS

© 2007 Spectacular Books

Designed by Brandon Downing

Selections previously published in *Chain, The DC Poetry Anthology, The Hat, Logopoeia, Poetry Daily, PoetsAgainsttheWar.org,* and *The Tangent.*

ANTIGONE was performed at the Small Press Traffic Literary Arts Center in San Francisco by Stacy Doris and Kevin Killian, in a production directed by Kevin Killian.

AT THE MET is a collaboration with the author of *The Minor Arcana.*

For Kid Rock/Total Freedom is set between January 2002 and April 2003.

PRINTED IN CANADA

ISBN 978-1-934200-01-8

FOR

KID

ROCK

TOTAL

FREEDOM

i	:	Antigone
ii	:	Mass Effects
iii	:	Lateox Dov
iv	:	Model States
v	:	At the Met

A drama, according to Freytag, is divided into five parts, or acts: **i**, exposition or in medias res; **ii**, history or backstory (rising action); **iii**, climax or crisis (turning point); **iv**, delay or consideration of possible courses of action (falling action); and **v**, denouement. A comedy is a drama in which the protagonist is better off at the end of the story than he or she was at the beginning; a tragedy is the opposite.

—Wikipedia, "Dramatic Structure"

i: Antigone

Greetings your brother is dead

—Whi—which

Both

—oh—o

I am sorry for your loss

—I understand

Yes h

—But I think

He died a

—What

Your brother died a

—Thank you bu

His heroi

—but not—Polyn—

Yes

—I thought—he oppose

He was

—He op

He was brought to freedom

—No he opposed you

We've taken char

—How ca

Here is his location

—What—wh

We've got sev

—I don't see h

At this point it

—You're not going t

At this ti

—But if you're in c

It's not nec

—Yes i

At this

—Yes it i

We're mov

—But you can't j

It's n

—Yes

It's

—Y

We're mo

—I'm go

No tha

—I'm going to

Tha

—You'll have to k

Gree

ii: Mass Effects

in two parts

- Ten studies, drawn from Wikipedia, in nationalism
  of the short 20th century (1914-1989)

- Mass Effects (as of 2003)

But the *length* of this path has to be endured, because, for one thing, each
moment is necessary; and further, each moment has to be *lingered* over, because
each is itself a complete individual shape, and one is only viewed in absolute
perspective when its determinateness is regarded as a concrete whole, or the
whole is regarded as uniquely qualified by that determination.

—G.W.F. Hegel, *Phenomenology of Spirit*

If we imagine it, does that bring it closer?
How many are imagining it

[meaning

scaling-down into the perceptible]

right now, and how?

mere affect

m a s

g r a v

1921

1923

1931

1934

1936

1939

1973

1975

Spain

1921

1941

1953

1963

1979

1980

1988

Iran

1918

1919

1922

1930

1942

1945

1947

1965

1971

India and Pakistan

1917

1933

1936

1948

1956

1967

1973

1979

1982

1987

Israel and Palestine

1927

1929

1931

1932

1937

1945

1949

1966

1989

China

1960

1965
1966

1967

1970

1979

Nigeria

1920

1924

1932

1964

1970

1973

Chile

1945

1949

1954

1973
1975
1976

1978

1986

Vietnam

1954

1958

1962

1965

1988

Algeria

1948

1955

1957

1965

1989

Colómbia

Aarhus United A/S — Abbey — Abbott Laboratories — Abertis Infraestructuras — ABIOMED — ABN AMRO — Abu Dhabi Co. (ADCO) — Abu Dhabi Marine Operating Company (ADMA-OPCO) — Abu Dhabi National Oil Company (ADNOC) — Abu Nidal Organization (ANO) — Abu Sayyaf Group (ASG) — Academy for Educational Development — Accenture — Accor — ACOM — Action Directe — Action for Southern Africa (ACTSA) — Action Without Borders — Adecco — Adidas-Salomon AG — ADNO — Adobe Systems — Advantest — Advisory Committee on Protection of the Sea — AEGON — AEON — Aerospace Corp. — AES — Aetna — al-Faran —Affiliated Computer Services — AFL-CIO — Afghanistan — AFLAC — Africa Action — Africa Confidential — Africa Research Bulletin — The African Academy of Sciences — African Affairs — African Community Publishing Trust — African Economic Research Consortium (AERC) — African Gender Institute — African Medical and Research Foundation (AMREF) — Agere Systems — AGF — Agilent Technologies — Agip — Agrilink Foods Inc. — Agua Bolivia — Ahl-e-Hadees — Aid for Northern Ireland — AIFUL — Air Products & Chemicals Inc. — Aisin Seiki — Ajinomoto — Akina Mama wa Afrika — Akzo Nobel — Alan Guttmacher Institute — Albania — Albanian National Army (ANA) — Albertsons — Alcan — Alcatel — Alcoa — Alcon Laboratories — Alex Boncayao Brigade (ABB) — Algeria — Algeti Wolves — Ali Suleiyman — Aliran — All Arctic Indigenous Youth Alliance — Alleanza Assicurazioni — Allergan — Alliance & Leicester — Alliance of Eritrean National Force — Alliance pour la resistance démocratique (ARD) — Alliant Techsystems Inc. — Allianz — Allied Democratic Forces (ADF) — Allied Domecq — Allied Irish Banks — AlliedSignal — Allstate — Alltel — Almanij — Altadis — ALTANA Group— Altera — Altria Group — AMAL — Amazon Watch — Amazon.com — Ambac Financial Group — Amcor — Amdocs — Amerada Hess Corp. — Ameren — American Association of University Women (AAUW) — American Civil Liberties Union (ACLU) — American Electric Power (AEP) — American Enterprise Institute — American Foreign Policy Council — American Express — American Foods Group Inc. — American International Group (AIG) — American International Oil & Gas Co. — American Israel Public Affairs Committee (AIPAC) — American Standard Cos. Inc. — AmerisourceBergen — Amersham —

Amgen — Amigos de la Tierra — Aminoil — Amn Araissi — Amnesty International — AMP Ltd. — AmSouth Bancorporation — Amvescap — Anadarko Petroleum Corp. — Analog Devices — Analysis and Technology Inc. — Angola — Anheuser-Busch — Ansar al-Islam — Anthem Heathcare — Anti-Imperialist International Brigade (AIIB) — Anti-Imperialist Territorial Nuclei (NTA) — Anti-Slavery International — AOL Time Warner — Aon Corp.— Apollo Group — Apple Computer Inc. — Applied Biosystems — Applied Materials — al-Aqsa Martyrs Brigade — Arab Petroleum Investments Corp. (API-CORP) — Arab Revolutionary Brigades — Arab Revolutionary Council — Arab Women's Solidarity Association (AWSA) — Arabian Oil Co. Ltd.— Aramark — Aramco Overseas Co. (Saudi Aramco) — Aramco Services Co. — Arcelor — Archer Daniels Midland — Archstone-Smith Trust — ARCO Qatar Inc. — Arewa People's Congress (Nigeria) — Argentina — Armed Islamic Group (GIA) — Armed Islamic Movement (AIM) — Armed Nuclei for Proletarian Autonomy — Armed Proletarian Nuclei — Armed Revolutionary Nuclei (ARN) — Armée pour la libération du Rwanda (ALIR) — Armenia — Armenian Secret Army for the Liberation of Armenia (ASALA) — Aruba — Asahi Glass — Asahi Kasei Corp. — 'Asbat al-Ansar — Ashland Oil Inc. — Ashmore and Cartier Islands — al-'Asifa — ASML Holding — Asociación ANAI — Asociación Guatemalteca para la Conservación Natural — ASSA ABLOY— Assicurazioni Generali — Associació Nereo, Preservador del Medi Ambient — Associated British Foods — Associated Country Women of the World — Associated Universities Inc. — Association for Progressive Communications (APC) — Association for Stimulating Know How (ASK) — Association for the Defense of the Nature and the Resources of Extremadura — Association for Women in Science — Association of Junior Leagues International Inc. — Association for Social Engineering, Research and Training (ASSERT) — AstraZeneca International — AT&T — AT&T Wireless Services — Athletes United for Peace — Atlantic Richfield Co. — Atlas Copco — Aum Shinrikyo — Aurora Foods Inc. — Australia — Austria — Automatic Data Processing Inc. (ADP) — AutoNation — Autoroutes du Sud de la France (ASF) — AutoZone — Aventis — Avery Dennison Corp. — Aviva — Avon Products Inc. — Avondale Industries Inc. — AXA Group — Azad Khalistan — Azerbaijan — B'Tselem: The Israeli

Information Center for Human Rights in the Occupied Territories —
BAA — Baader-Meinhof Gang — Babbar Khalsa Force — al-Badhr
Mujahedin — Baker Institute of Public Policy — BAE Systems — The
Bahamas — Bahrain — Bahrain Aviation Fueling Co. (BAFCO) —
Bahrain National Gas Co. (Banagas) — The Bahrain National Oil
Company (BANOCO) — Bahrain Petroleum Co. (BAPCO) — Baker
Hughes Inc. — Baker Island — Banc One — Banca Antonveneta —
Banca Fideuram — Banca Intesa — Banca Monte dei Paschi di Siena
(BMPS) — Banca Nazionale del Lavoro — Banco Bilbao Vizcaya
Argentaria (BBVA) — Banco Comercial Portúgues (BCP) — Banco
Espirito Santo (BES) — Banco Popular Español — Banco Sabadell —
Banco Santander Central Hispano (SCH)— Bangladesh — Bank
Information Center (BIC) — Bank of America — Bank of Montreal
(BMO)— Bank of New York — Bank of Nova Scotia Berhad
(Scotiabank) — Bank of Yokohama Ltd. — Banknorth Group —
Barbados — Barclays — BARD — Barr Laboratories Inc. — Barrick
Gold Corp. — BASF Corp. — Basque Homeland and Liberty (ETA) —
Bass Enterprise Production Co. — Bassas da India — Bath Holding
Corp. — Battelle Memorial Institute — Bavarian Liberation Army —
Baxter International — Bayer — BB&T — Blue Diamond Mining
Corp. (BDM) — BEA Systems Inc. — Bear, Stearns & Co. Inc.—
Bechtel Group Inc. — BD (Becton, Dickinson and Co.) — Bed Bath &
Beyond — Beiersdorf — Belarus — Belgium — Belize — Bell Atlantic
Corp. — BellSouth — Benin — Berkshire Hathaway Inc. — Bermuda —
Best Buy — BEWAG — BG Group — Bhinderanwala Tiger Force —
BHP Billiton Ltd. — Bhutan — Biogen — Biomet Inc. — Biovail — BJ
Services Co. — Black Mamba — Black September — BMC Software
Inc. — BMW — BNP Paribas — BO (Kuwait) Ltd. — BOC Group —
Boeing Co. — Bolivia — Bombardier — Boots Group — Booz Allen
Hamilton Inc. — Borden Foods Corp. — Bosnia and Herzegovina —
Boston Properties Inc. — Boston Scientific Corp. — Botswana —
Bouvet Island — Bouygues — BP — Bangladesh Rural Advance
Commission (BRAC) — Brambles Industries Ltd. — Brascan Corp. —
Brazil — Breton Liberation Front — Breton Revolutionary Army —
Bretton Woods Project — Bridgestone Corp. — Brigades of the
Martyr Abdallah al-Hudhaifi — Brigate Rosse — Bristol-Myers

Squibb Co. — British American Tobacco — British Gas Co. — British Indian Ocean Territory — The Britich Land Co. — British Sky Broadcasting Group — British Virgin Islands — Broadcom Corp. — Brookfield Properties — Brookings Institution — The Brotherhood — Brown-Forman Corp. — Brunei — BT Group — BTG Inc. — Bulgaria — Burkina Faso — Burlington Resources — Burma — Burundi — Cablevision Systems Corp. — Cadbury Schweppes — Cadence Design Systems — California Institute of Technology — Caltex Petroleum Corp. — Cambodia — Cambodian Freedom Fighters (CFF) — Cameroon — Campbell Soup Co. — Canada — Canadian Commercial Corp. — Canadian Imperial Bank of Commerce (CIBC) — Canadian Institute for Environmental Law and Policy (CIELAP) — Canadian National Railway — Canadian Natural Resources Ltd. — Canadian Nature Federation — Canadian Pacific Railway — Canandaigua Brands Inc. — Canon Inc. — Cap Gemini — Cape Verde — Capital One — Capitalia — Caprivi Liberation Front — Captive Daughters — Cardinal Health Inc. — CARE International — Caribbean Conservation Association — The Carlyle Group — Carnival plc — Carrefour — Carter Center — Casino Guichard-Perrachon — Caterpillar — Cathay Pacific Airways — Catholic Reaction Force (CRF) — Cato Institute — Cayman Islands — Celesio — Cellules Communistes Combattantes — Cendant Corp. — Center for a Sustainable Coast — Center for Applied Biodiversity Science — Center for Defense Information — Center for Economic and Social Rights — Center for Institute for Health Information — Center for International Law — Center for Reproductive and Family Health — Center for Reproductive Law and Policy (CRLP) — Center for Strategic and International Studies — Centex Corp. — Central African Republic — Centre for Sustainable Design — Centre on Housing Rights and Evictions (COHRE) — Centrica — Centro de Derecho Ambiental y de los Recursos Naturales (CEDARENA) — Centro de Estudios Agrarios y Ambientales (CEA) — Centro Ecuatoriano de Derecho Ambiental (CEDA) — Centro Mexicano de Derecho Ambiental (CEMDA) — CenturyTel Inc. — CFP — Chad — Charles Schwab & Co. — Charles Stark Draper Laboratory Inc. — Charter One Financial Inc. — Chelsea Milling Co. — Cheung Kong

Holdings Ltd. — Cheung Kong Infrastructure Holdings Ltd. —
Chevron Corp. — Chevron Overseas Petroleum Inc. —
ChevronTexaco — Chile — China — China Youth Development
Foundation — Chinese Petroleum Corp. — Chiquita Brands
International Inc. — Chiron Corp. — Christian Dior — Christmas
Island — Chubb Corp. — CHUBU Electric Power Co. Inc. — Chugai
Pharmaceutical Co. Ltd. — The Chugoku Electric Power Co. Inc. —
Chukaku-Ha — Ciba Spezialitätenchemie Holding — Center for
International Earth Science Information Network (CIESIN) — Cigna
— Cincinnati Financial Corp. — Cinergy — Cintas Corp. — Cisco
Systems Inc. — CIT Group Inc. — Citigroup — Citizens
Communications — Citrix Systems Inc. — Clear Channel
Communications — Clipperton Island — Clorox — Cloud Forest
Alive — CLP Holdings — Clubul Ecologic UNESCO Pro Natura —
CNA Financial — National Council of Maubere Resistance (CNRM)
— National Council of Timorese Resistance (CNRT) — Coach —
Coca-Cola Enterprises Inc. — Coca-Cola HBC — Cocos (Keeling)
Islands — Coles Myer Ltd. — Colgate-Palmolive Co. — Colómbia —
Comcast — Comerica — Committee for International Cooperation in
National Research in Demography (CICRED) — Commandos of the
November 95 Anarchist Group — Commerzbank — Committee for
Eastern Turkistan — Committee for the Defense of Legitimate
Rights — Communist Party of India (Marxist-Leninist) —
Communist Party of Nepal (Maoist) — Comoros — Compagnie
Financière Richemont SA — Compañía Española de Petróleos SA
(CEPSA) — Compass Bancshares Inc. — Compass Group —
Computer Associates International Inc. — Computer Sciences Corp.
— ConAgra Foods Inc. — Concord EFS Inc. — Congo, Democratic
Republic of the — ConocoPhillips Co. — Conseil national pour la
défense de la démocratie (CNDD) — Consejo Ibérico para la Defensa
de la Naturaleza — Consejo Latinoamericano de Ciencias Sociales
(CLASCO) — Conservation Council of South Australia (CCSA) —
Conservation Council of Western Australia Inc. (CCWA) —
Conservation International — Consolidated Edison Inc. —
Constellation Energy Group Inc. — Consultative Group on
International Agricultural Research (CGIAR) — Cook Islands —

Cooper Industries Inc. — Coral Sea Islands — Corning Inc. — Corporate Watch — Cosmote — Costa Rica — Costco Wholesale Corp. — Côte d'Ivoire — Countrywide Financial Corp. — Cox Communications — Crédit Agricole Groupe — Credit Suisse Group — CRH — Croatia — CSX — Cuba — Cubic Corp. — Cultural Survival — CVS/pharmacy — CXO Ltd. — Cyprus — Czech Republic — Dai Nippon Printing Co. Ltd. — Daiichi Pharmaceutical Co. Ltd. — Daikin Industries Ltd. — Daily Mail and General Trust — DaimlerChrysler — Daiwa House Industry Co. Ltd. — Daiwa Securities Group Inc. — Dal Khalsa — Dampskibsselskabet AF — Dampskibsselskabet Svenborg — Danaher Corp. — Danske Bank — Dassault Systemes — Day & Zimmermann Inc. Group — Dayak — DBS Group Holdings Ltd. — Dean Foods Co. — Deere & Co. — Degussa Corp. — Del Monte Foods — Dell Inc. — Delphi — Democratic Front for the Liberation of Palestine (DFLP) — Democratic Karen Burmese Army (DKBA) — Denmark — Denso Corp. — Dentsu Inc. — Derechos Human Rights — Desert Research Foundation of Namibia — Deutsche Bank Group — Deutsche Boerse — Deutsche Erdöl AG — Deutsche Lufthansa — Deutsche Post — Deutsche Telekom — Development Alternatives with Women for a New Era (DAWN) — Devon Energy Corp. — Devrimci Sol (Revolutionary Left) — Dexia — Diageo — Direct Action Against Drugs (DADD) — DirecTV Group — Dixons Group — Djibouti — Djibouti Youth Movement — DnB Holding Norway — Dole Food Co. Inc. — Dollar General Corp. — Dominica — Dominican Republic — Dominion — Dow Chemical Co. — Dow Jones & Co. Inc. — DSM Group — DST Systems Inc. — DTE Energy Co. — Duke Energy Corp. — Duke Realty Corp. — Dukhtaran-e-Millat — DuPont — DynCorp International — E.ON — The E.W. Scripps Co. — The Earth Council — Earth Island Institute — EarthRights International — Earth Society Foundation — Earth Summit Watch — Earth Times Foundation — Earthtrust Inc. — Earthwatch Institute — Earthgrains Co. — Earthscan — East Timor — Eastern Shan State Army (ESSA) — Eastman Kodak Co. — Eaton Corp. — Ebay — EC/UNFPA Initiative for Reproductive Health in Asia — EchoStar Communications — Ecolab Inc. — Economic Policy Institute — Ecuador —

Edison International — EFG Eurobank Ergasias — EG&G Inc. — Egypt —Egyptian Organization for Human Rights (EOHR) — Eisai Inc. — Ejército Popular Boricua (Macheteros) — Ejército Popular Revolucionario (EPR) — El Salvador — Eleanor Roosevelt Center at Val-Kill — Electrabel Belgium — Electricidade de Portugal Group (EDP) — Electrolux — Electronic Arts (EA) — Electronic Data Systems Corp. (EDS) — Elf Aquitaine — Elf Atochem — Elf Petroleum Qatar — Eli Lilly and Co. — Ellalan Force — Ejército de Liberación Nacional (ELN) — Emanuel Rodriguez Patriotic Front (FPMR) — Emap — EMC Corp. — Emerson Electric Co. — Empowerment for African Sustainable Development (EASD)— Enbridge Inc. — EnCana Corp. — Endesa — Enel — Eni SpA — Enron — ENSCO International — Entergy Corp. — Environment Liaison Center International (ELCI) — Environmental Defense Fund — EOG Resources Inc. — Ethniki Organosis Kyprion Agoniston (EOKA) — Equality Now — Equatorial Guinea — Equifax — Equity Office Properties Trust — Equity Residential — Eritrea — Eritrean Democratic Liberation Movement — Eritrean Islamic Jihad Movement — Eritrean Liberation Front—Revolutionary Council (ELF-RC) — Eritrean People's Liberation Front (EPLF) — Ejército Revolucionario del Pueblo (ERP) — Erste Bank Group — Essilor International — Estée Lauder Inc. — Estonia — Ethiopia — Europa Island — EUROPARC Federation — European Aeronautic Defence and Space Co. (EADS) — European Centre for Nature Conservation — European Chemicals Bureau — Euzkadi Ta Askatasuna (ETA) — Everest Re Group Ltd. — Executive Outcomes — Exelon Corp. — Forces armées rwandaises (ex-FAR) — Expedia Inc. — Expeditors International of Washington Inc. — Express Scripts Inc. — ExxonMobil Corp. — National Armed Forces for the Liberation of East Timor (FALINTIL) — Falkland Islands (Islas Malvinas) — Family Care International — Family Dollar Stores Inc. — Family Health International (FHI) — Fannie Mae — FANUC Robotics — Farabundo Martí National Liberation Front (FMLN) — al-Faran — al-Fatah — Faroe Islands — Fast Retailing Co. Ltd. — Fatah Revolutionary Council — Fauna and Flora International (FFI) — Farley's & Sathers Candy Co. Inc. — Federated Department Stores Inc. — Federation of

American Women's Clubs Overseas Inc. (FAWCO) — Federation of Associations of Canadian Tamils (FACT) — FedEx — Fiat Group — Fidelity National Financial — 15 May Organization (Abu Ibrahim Faction) — Fifth Third Bancorp — Fighting Islamic Group (FIG) — Fiji — Finland — Finmeccanica Inc. — First Data Corp. — First Tennessee National Bank Association— FirstEnergy Cos. — Fiserv — FleetBoston Financial — Flextronics International — Flowers Industries Inc. — Fluor Corp. — FMC Corp. — Fondo de las Américas — FoodFirst Information and Action Network (FIAN International) — Force 17 — Forces armées du peuple (FAP) — Forces de libération nationale (FALINA) — Forces nationales de libération (FNL) — Forces pour la défense de la démocratie (FDD) — Ford Motor Co. — Foreign Policy Institute — FöreningsSparbanken — Forest Laboratories Inc. — Fortis Belgium — Fortum Corp. — Fortune Brands Inc. — Forum for the Future — Foster Farms — Foster's Group Ltd. — Fox Entertainment Group — FPL Group Inc. — France — Franklin Resources Inc. — Fraxia Midheniston — Freddie Mac — Free Papua Movement (OPM) — Freedom House Inc. — French Guiana — French Polynesia — French Southern and Antarctic Lands — Fresenius Medical Care — Revolutionary Front for an Independent East Timor (FRETILIN) — Friends of the Earth — Frito-Lay — Front contre l'occupation tutsie (FLOT) — Front de Libération Nationale — Front Line — Front pour la libération nationale (FROLINA) — Fuerzas Armadas Liberación Nacional Puertoriqueña (FALN) — Fuerzas Armadas Revolucionarias de Colómbia—Ejército del Pueblo (FARC-EP) — Fuji Photo Film Co. Ltd. — Fujisawa Pharmaceutical Co. Ltd. — Fujitsu Ltd. — Fundación Desarrollo Sostenido (FUNDESO) — Fundación Príncipe de Asturias — Gabon — Gallaher Group Inc. — al-Gama'a al-Islamiyya — The Gambia, the Republic of — Gannett Co. — Gap Inc. — Garmin Ltd. — Gas Natural SDG — Gazprom — Gencorp Inc. — Genentech Inc. — General Dynamics Corp. — General Electric Co. — General Federation of Women's Clubs — General Growth Properties Inc. — General Mills Inc. — General Motors Corp. — General Property Trust — Genuine Parts Co. — Genzyme General — George Weston Ltd. — Georgia — Georgia-Pacific Corp. — Gerakin Aceh Merdeka (GAM) — Germany — Getty

Oil Co. — Ghana — Gibraltar — Gilead Sciences — Gillette Co. — GlaxoSmithKline — The Global Alliance for Women's Health (GAWH) — Global Fund for Women — Global Witness — GlobalSantaFe Corp. — Globe Oil and Refining Co. — Glorioso Islands — God's Army — Gold Kist Inc. — Golden West Financial Corp. — Goldman Sachs Group Inc. — Granada — Great-West Lifeco Inc. — Greece — Green Alliance — Green Earth Foundation — Green Front of Iran Inc. — Green Line — Greenland — GreenPoint Financial Corp. — Grenada — Groupe Bruxelles Lambert (GBL) — Groupe Danone — Groupe UCB Belgium — Grupo de Resistencia Antifascista Primero de Octubre (GRAPO) — Grupo FCC — Grupo Ferrovial — GTE Corp. — GTSI Corp. — Guadeloupe — Guam — Guatemala — Gucci Group — Guernsey — Guidant Corp. — Guinea — Guinea-Bissau — Gulf Oil L.P.— Gulf Kuwait Co. — Gulfstream Aerospace Corp. — GUS plc — Guyana — H&R Block — H. Lundbeck — H.J. Heinz Co. — Haiti — Haitian Movement for Rural Development (MHDR) — Halliburton Co. — HAMAS (Islamic Resistance Movement) — Hang Seng Bank Ltd. — Hanson & Co. — Harakat ul-Ansar (HUA) — Harakat ul-Jihad-I-Islami (HUJI) — Harakat ul-Jihad-I-Islami/Bangladesh (HUJI-B) — Harakat ul-Mujahidin (HUM) — Harken Energy Corp. — Harley-Davidson — Harrah's Entertainment — Harris Corp. — The Hartford Financial Services Group Inc. — Harvard University — The Hauser Center for Nonprofit Organizations — Hawari Group — HBOS — HCA Inc. — Health Net — Heard Island and McDonald Islands — Heineken — Heineken International — Hellenic Telecommunications Organization — Henderson Land Development Co. Ltd. — Henkel — Hennes & Mauritz (H&M) — Hensel Phelps Construction Co. — Heritage Foundation — Hermès International — Hershey Foods Corp. — Hewlett-Packard — Hilton Hotels Corp. — Hitachi Ltd. — Hizb ul-Mujahidin (HM) — Hizballa (Kuwait) — Hizballah (Bahrain) — Hizballah (Lebanon) — Hizballah al-Khalji — Hizb-i Islami Gulbuddin (HIG) — Hizb-i Wahdat (The Unity Party) — Hizbullah (Turkey) — Holcim Inc. — Home Depot U.S.A. Inc. — Honda Motor Co. — Honduras — Honeywell International — Hong Kong and China Gas Co. Ltd. — Hongkong Electric Holdings Ltd. — Hoover

Institution on War, Revolution, and Peace — Hormel Foods Corp. — Horton Inc. — Hotels.com — Howe-Baker Engineering Inc. — Howland Island — HSBC Holdings — Hudson Institute — Hudson City Bancorp Inc. — Human Rights Advocates (HRA) — Human Rights Foundation of Turkey — Human Rights in China — Human Rights Internet — Human Sciences Research Council of South Africa — Humana Inc. — The Hungarian Oil & Gas Company Ltd. — Hungary — The Hunger Project — Huntington Bancshares Inc. — Husky Energy Inc. — Hutchison Whampoa Ltd. — HypoVereinsbank — Iberdrola — IBM Corp. — IBP Inc. — Iceland — IDEC Pharmaceuticals — IGC Internet — Ikhwan-ul-Mussalmin — Illinois Tool Works Inc. (ITW) — Imperial Oil Ltd. — Imperial Tobacco Group — IMS Health Inc. — Inco Ltd. — Indev — India — Inditex Group — Indonesia — The Indonesia Human Rights Campaign (TAPOL) — Infineon Technologies — ING Groep— Ingersoll—Rand Co. Ltd. — Institute of Development Studies (IDS) — Institute of Social Studies Trust (ISST) — Instituto de Derecho y Economía Ambiental — Instituto de Desarrollo y Medio Ambiente — Instituto del Tercer Mundo (ITeM) — Instituto Social y Politico de la Mujer (ISPM) — Intel Corp. — InterAction — InterActiveCorp (IAC) — Interahamwe — Interbrew Belgium — InterContinental Hotels Group — Intercooperation — Interhemispheric Resource Center (IRC) — Intermediate Technology DevelopmentGroup — International Alert — International Association on Water Quality — International Center for Research on Women (ICRW) — International Centre for Integrated Mountain Development (ICIMOD) — International Centre for Research in Agroforestry (ICRAF) — International Commission of Jurists — International Community of Women Living with HIV/AIDS (ICW) — International Council of Jewish Women (ICJW) — International Development Research Centre (IDRC) — International Federation of University Women — International Game Technology (IGT) — International Helsinki Federation for Human Rights (IHF) — International Human Rights Association of American Minorities (IHRAAM) — International Human Rights Law Group — International Institute for Sustainable Development (IISD) — International Islamic Front for Jihad Against the Jews and Crusaders — International Justice Group — International Multifoods Corp. — International Octane Ltd. — International Paper Co. — International Petroleum Industry Environmental Conservation Association — International Planned Parenthood Federation (IPPF) — International Revolutionary Action Group (GARI) — International Rivers Network — International Shipholding Corp. Inc. — International Sikh Youth Federation (ISYF) — International South Group Network (ISGN) — International Water Management Institute (IWMI) — International Wildlife Coalition (IWC) — International Women's Health Coalition (IWHC) — International Women's Tribune Centre (IWTC) — International Work Group for Indigenous Affairs (IWGIA) — Interpublic Group of Companies — Interstate Bakeries Corp. — Intuit Inc. — Investors Group Inc. — Iparretarrak (IK) — Iran — Iranian National Front — Iranian Oil Participants Ltd. — Iraq — Iraqi National Accord (INA) — Iraqi National Congress (INC) — IRC International Water and Sanitation Centre — Ireland — Iricon Agency Ltd. — Irish National Liberation Army (INLA) — Irish Republican Army (IRA) — Isatabu Freedom Movement (IFM) — Isis International Manila — Islamic Army of Aden (IAA) — Islamic Great Eastern Raiders Front — Islamic International Peacekeeping Brigade (IIPB) — Islamic Jihad for the Liberation of Palestine — Islamic Liberation Army (AIS) — Islamic Movement for Change — Islamic Movement of Uzbekistan (IMU) — Islamic Movement Organization — Islamic Salvation Army — Islamic Salvation Front (FIS) — Israel — Italy — ITOCHU International Inc. (III) — Ito-Yokado Co. Ltd. — ITT Corp. — al-Ittihad al-Islami (AIAI) — Iwokrama International Centre for Rain Forest Conservation and Development — J Sainsbury — JCPenney — The J.M. Smucker Co. — JPMorgan Chase & Co. — Jabil Circuit Inc. — Jaish-e-Mohammed (JEM) — al-Jama'a al-Islamiyya al-Muqatilah bi-Libya — Jamaat ul-Fuqra — Jamaica — Jamaica Conservation and Development Trust — Jamat-e-Islami — Jamiat ul-Mujahidin (JUM) — Jamiat-e-Ahl-e-Hadees — Jammu and Kashmir Liberation Front (JKLF) — Jan Mayen — Janus Capital Group — Japan — Japan Oil Development Co. (JODCO) - Japan Petroleum Trading Co. Ltd. — Japan Petroleum Exploration Co. Ltd. (JapEx) — Jardine Matheson

Ltd. — Jarvis Island — JDS Uniphase Corp. — Jefferson-Pilot Securities — Jemaah Islamiya (JI) — Jersey — Jeune Afrique — JFE Holdings Inc. — John Hancock Financial Services — Johns Hopkins University — Johnson & Johnson — Johnson Controls Inc. — Johnson Electric Holdings Ltd. — Johnston Atoll — Joint Center for Political and Economic Affairs — Jones Apparel Group Inc. — Jordan — Juan de Nova Island — Juniper Networks Inc. — Kach — Kachin Defense Army (KDA) — Kachin Independence Organization (KIO) — Kaiser-Hill Co. — Kansai Electric Power Co. Inc. (KEPCO) — Kao Corp. — Karen National Defense Organization (KNDO) — Karen National Union (KNU) — Kazakhstan — KBC Bancassurance Holding Belgium — KDDI Corp. — Keebler Foods Co. — Kellogg Brown & Root — Kennedy School of Government — Kenya — Kerr—McGee Corp. — Keycorp Ltd. — Keyence Corp. — Keyspan — Keystone Foods — Khalistan Commando Force (KCF) — Khalistan Liberation Front — Khalistan Liberation Tiger Force — Khalistan National Army — Khmer Rouge — Kimberly-Clark Corp. — Kimco Realty Corp. — Kinder Morgan Inc. — Kingfisher Airlines — Kingman Reef — Kinki Nippon Railway — Kiribati — Kirin Brewery Co. Ltd. — KLA-Tencor Corp. — Knight-Ridder Inc. — Kohl's Illinois Inc. — Komala — Komatsu Ltd. — Koninklijke Ahold — Korea, North — Korea, South — Korea International Volunteer Organization — Kosovo Liberation Army (KLA) — Kraft Foods Inc. — The Kroger Co. — Ku Klux Klan — Kumpulan Mujahidin Malaysia (KMM) — Kurdish Democratic Party of Iran (KDPI) — Kurdish Human Rights Project — Kurdistan Democratic Party (KDP) — Kurdistan Workers' Party (PKK) — Kuwait — Kuwait Foreign Petroleum Exploration Co. (KUFPEC) — Kuwait National Petroleum Co. (KNPC) — Kuwait Oil Co. (KOC) — Kuwait Oil Tanker Co. (KOTC) — Kuwait Petroleum Corp. (KPC) — Kuwait Petroleum International (KPI) — Kuwait Shell Development Co. Ltd. — Kyocera Corp. — Kyrgyzstan — Kyushu Electric Power Co. Inc. — L'air Liquide — L'Oréal — L-3 Communications Holdings — La Cosa Nostra — Laboratory Corporation of America Holdings — Lafarge Group — Lagardère — Lamar Advertising Co. — Lance Inc. — Land O'Lakes Inc. — Land Securities Group — Laos — Lashkar i-Jhangvi — Lashkar-i-Tayyiba —

Latvia — Lautaro Faction of the United Popular Action Movement (MAPU/L) — Lautaro Popular Rebel Forces (FRPL) — Lautaro Youth Movement (MJL) — Lavan Petroleum Co. — Lebanese Armed Revolutionary Faction (LARF) — Lebanon — Lee Chang Yung Chemical Industry Corp. — Legal & General Group — Legg Mason — Leggett & Platt Inc. — Lehman Brothers Holdings — Lennar Corp. — Les Mongoles — Lesotho — Lexmark International Inc. — Li & Fung Ltd. — Liberation Army of the Islamic Sanctuaries — Liberation Tigers of Tamil Eelam (LTTE) — Liberia — Liberty Media Corp. — Libya — Liechtenstein — Liga de Defensa del Medio Ambiente (LIDEMA) — Limited Brands — Lincoln Financial — Linde — Linear Technology — Lithuania — Litton Industries Inc. — Liz Claiborne Inc. — Lloyds TSB Group — LM Ericsson — Loblaw Cos. Ltd. — Lockheed Martin Corp. — Loews — Lord's Resistance Army (LRA) — Los Macheteros — Lowe's — Loyalist Volunteer Force (LVF) — Lucent Technologies — Luxembourg — Luxottica Group — LVMH Louis Vuitton Moët Hennessy — M&T Bank Corp. — Macau — Macedonia, The Former Yugoslav Republic of — Macquarie Bank Ltd. — Macquarie Infrastructure Group (MIG) — Madagascar — Maersk Inc. — Maersk Oil Qatar Co. — Magna International Inc. — Magyar Olaj Gazi (MOL) — Maktab al-Khidamat (MAK) — Malaita Eagles Force (MEF) — Malawi — Malaysia — Maldives — Mali — Malta — Man Group — Man, Isle of — Management & Training Corp. — ManTech International Corp. — Manulife Financial — Maoist Communist Centre (MCC) — Marathon Oil Corp. — Marie Stopes International — Marks & Spencer Group — Marriott International Inc. — Mars Inc. — Marsh & McLennan Companies — Marshall & Ilsley Corp. — Marshall Islands — Martinique — Martyrs of Tal al-Za'atar — Marubeni Corp. — Marvell Technology Group Ltd. — Masco Corp. — Mason & Hanger—Silas Mason Co. Inc. — Massachusetts Institute of Technology — Matsushita Electric Industrial Co. Ltd. — Matsushita Electric Works Ltd. — Mattel Inc. — Mau Mau — Mauritania — Mauritius — Maxim Integrated Products — The May Department Stores Co. — Mayi-Mayi — Mayotte — MBIA Inc. — MBNA Corp. — McCormick & Co. Inc. — McDermott International Inc. — McDonald's — The McGraw-Hill Companies — MCI Communications — McKee

Foods Corp. — McKesson — MeadWestvaco — Meccan Group — Mediaset — MedImmune Inc. — Mediobanca — Mediolanum — Medtronic Inc. — Mellon Financial Corp. — Merck & Co. Inc. — Merck KGaA — Merrill Lynch & Co. Inc. — Methanex Corp. — MetLife — Mexico — MGIC Investment Corp. — MGM Mirage — Michelin Group— Microchip Technology Inc. — Micron Technology Inc. — Micronesia, Federated States of — Microsoft Corp. — Middle-Core Faction — Midway Atoll — Milken Institute — Millea Holdings Inc. — Millennium Pharmaceuticals Inc. — Minnesota Patriots Council — Minority Rights Group International — MITRE Corp. — Mitretek Systems Inc. — Mitsubishi Companies — Mitsui Group — Mitsui Sumitomo Insurance Co. Ltd. — Mizuho Financial Group Inc. — Materials and Manufacturing Ontatio (MMO) — Mobil Oil Qatar — Mobil Qatar Gas Inc. — Mohajir Qaumi Movement (MQM) — Mohawk Industries Inc. — Moldova — Molex — Monaco — Mong Tai Army (MTA) — Mongolia — Monsanto Co. — Montserrat — Moody's Investors Service — Morazanist Patriotic Front (FPM) — Morgan Stanley — Moro Islamic Liberation Front (MILF) — Moro National Liberation Front (MNLF) — Moroccan Islamic Combatant Group (GICM) — Morocco — Morrison Knudsen Corp. — Mothaidda Quami Movement (MQM) — Motor Oil Hellas — Motorola Inc. — Mott's Inc. — Mouvement de libération congolais (MLC) — Movement of Democratic Forces in the Casamance (MFDC) — Movimento Sociale Italiano — Movimiento de Liberación Nacional — Mozambique — MS Nepal — Münchener Rück — Mujahedin-e Khalq Organization (MEK or MKO) — Murata Manufacturing Co. Ltd. — Murphy Oil Corp. — Muslim Brotherhood — Muslim Iranian Student's Society — Muslims Against Global Oppression (MAGO) — Muttahida Jihad Council (MJC) — Muttahida Quami Movement (MQM) — Myanmar National Democratic Alliance Army (MNDAA) — Mylan Laboratories Inc. — Nabisco Holdings Corp. — Nabors Industries Ltd. — Namibia — Namibia Nature Foundation — Namibian Economic Policy Research Unit (NEPRU) — NASSCO Holdings Inc. — Natexis Banques Populaires — National Army for the Liberation of Uganda (NALU) — National Bank of Greece — National Center for Policy Analysis — National Center for Nonprofit Boards — National Commerce

Financial Corp. — National Committee for the Liberation and Defense of Albanian Lands (KKCMTSH) — National Council of Resistance of Iran (NCRI) — National Councils for Sustainable Development — National Front for the Liberation of Corsica — National Grid — National Ground Water Association — National Iranian Gas Export Co. (NIGEC) — National Iranian Oil Co. (NIOC) — National Liberation Army (ELN-Colombia) — National Liberation Army (ELN-Bolivia) — National Liberation Army of Iran (NLA) — National Liberation Front of Kurdistan (ERNK) — National Patriotic Front of Liberia (NPFL) — National Petrochemical Co. (NPC) — National Semiconductor Corp. — National United Front of Arakan (NUFA) — National Wildlife Federation (NWF) — Nationwide Financial Services — Natural Resources Defense Council (NRDC) — The Nature Conservancy — Nauru, the Republic of — Navassa Island — NEC Corp. — Nepal — Nestlé — NetAid — Netherlands — Netherlands Antilles — Netherlands Interdisciplinary Demographic Institute (NIDI) — Network Appliance Inc. — Network of Foundations and Nonprofit Organizations — New Caledonia — New Irish Republican Army (NIRA *or* Real IRA) — New Mon State Party (NMSP) — New People's Army (NPA) — New Red Brigades/ Communist Combatant Party (BR-PCC) — New York Community Bancorp — The New York Times Co. — New Zealand — Newell Rubbermaid — Newmont Mining Corp. — Newport News Shipbuilding — News Corp. — Nextel Communications — Nicaragua — Nichols Research Corp. — Nidec Corp. — Niger — Nigeria — Nike — Nikko Cordial Corp. — Nintendo of America Inc. — Nippon Express — Nippon Oil Corp. — Nippon Steel Corp. — Nippon Telegraph and Telephone Corp. (NTT) — Nippon Unipac Holding — Nippon Yusen Kaisha (NYK Line) — NiSource Inc. — Nissan Motor Co. Ltd. — Nissho Iwai — Nitto Denko Corp. — Niue — Nokia Finland — Nomura Holdings — Nordea — Norfolk Island — Norfolk Southern Corp. — Norsk Hydro Norway — Nortel Networks — North Fork Bancorporation — Northern Alliance — Northern Mariana Islands — Northern Rock — Northern Trust Corp. — Northrop Grumman Corp. — Norway — Novartis — Novellus Systems Inc. — Novo Nordisk — NTT Data Corp. — NTT DoCoMo Inc. — Nucleus

Faction — Nucor Corp. — NVIDIA Corp. — OCBC Bank — Occidental Petroleum Corp. — Occidental Petroleum of Qatar Ltd. — Occidental/Gulf — Office Depot Inc. — Ohio Valley Electric Corp. (OVEC) — Ohm Corp. — Oji Paper Co. Ltd. — Old Republic International Corp. — Olin Corp. — Olivetti — Olympus Optical — Oman — Oman Oil Co. (OOC) — Omnicom Group Inc. — OMRON Corp. — OneWorld.net — Ono Pharmaceutical Co. Ltd. — Oracle Corp. — Orange Volunteers — The Order — Ordine Nuovo (New Order) — Organisasi Papua Merdeka (OPM) — Organisation of Iranian People's Fedaian Majority (OIPFM) — Organization for Defending Victims of Violence (ODVV) — Organization of the Oppressed on Earth — Oriental Land Co. Ltd. — ORIX Corp. — Orkla Group — Orly Group — Osaka Gas Co. Ltd. — Oshkosh Truck Corp. — Oxfam International — PACCAR Inc. — Pacific Institute for Women's Health (PIWH) — Pakistan — Palau — Palestinian Islamic Jihad (PIJ) — Palestine Liberation Front (PLF) — Palestine Liberation Organization (PLO) — Palmyra Atoll — Pan-Pacific and South-East Asia Women's Association International — Panama — Panos Institute — Papua New Guinea — Paracel Islands — Paraguay — Parker Hannifin Corp. — Parrex — Partex Gas Corp. — Parti pour la libéra-tion du peuple hutu (PALIPEHUTU) — Participations and Explorations Corp. — Partido Democratico Popular Revolucionario (PDPR) — Party of Allah — Party of Democratic Kampuchea — Party of God — Patriotic Union of Kurdistan (PUK) — Pauley Petroleum Inc. — Paychex Inc. — Peabody Coal Co. — Peace Corps — Pearson — Pennzoil-Quaker State Co. — Pennzoil Qatar Oil Co. — People Against Gangsterism and Drugs (PAGAD) — People & Planet — People's Liberation Army (PLA) Ireland — People's Liberation Army of Kurdistan (ARGK) — People's Mujahedin of Iran (PMOI) — People's Republican Army (PRA) — People's Union for Civil Liberties (PUCL) — Peoples' War Group (PWG) [India] — Peoples' War Group (PWG) [Nepal] — PeopleSoft — Pepco Holdings Inc. — Pepsi Bottling Group Inc. — PepsiCo Inc. — Perdue Farms Inc. — Pernod Ricard — Peru — Peter Kiewit Sons' Inc. — Petro-Canada — Petrochemical Industries Co. (PIC) — Petroleum Development Oman Ltd. (PDO) — Petroliam Nasional Berhad (PETRONAS)— PetroLube

— Petromin Lubricating Oil Co. (Petrolube) — Petromin Lubricating Oil Refining Co. (Luberef) — Peugeot — Peuple en armes pour la libération du Rwanda (PALIR) — Pfizer Inc. — PG&E Co. — Philippines — Philip Morris International — Phillips Petroleum Co. — Physicians for Social Responsibility — Pilgrim's Pride Corp. — Pillsbury Co. — Pinault-Printemps-Redoute — Pioneer Foods Inc. — Pitcairn Islands — Pitney Bowes Inc. — Placer Dome Inc. — Plum Creek Timber Co. Inc. — PNC Financial Services Group — Poland — PopNet — Popular Front for the Liberation of Palestine (PFLP) — Popular Front for the Liberation of Palestine-General Command (PFLP-GC) — Popular Front for the Liberation of Palestine-Special Command (PFLP-SC) — Popular Liberation Forces (FPL) — Popular Revolutionary Vanguard — Popular Struggle Front (PSF) — Population Action International (PAI) — Population Services International Inc. (PSI) — Porsche — Portugal — Power Financial Corp. — PPG Industries — PPL Corp. — Praxair Technology Inc. — Preussag A.G. — Principal Financial Services Inc. — Pro-Fac Cooperative Inc. — Procter & Gamble — Progress Energy — Progressive Casualty Insurance Co. — Progressive Policy Institute — ProLogis — Promise Technology Inc. — Pro Natura (Swiss League for the Protection of Nature) — ProPoor — Proutist Universal — Provisional Irish Republican Army (PIRA *or* Provos) — Prudential Insurance Company of America — Prudential Financial — Public Service Enterprise Group Inc. — Public Services International (PSI) — Public Storage Inc. — Publicis — Puerto Rico — Puka Inti — Pullman-Kellogg — Pulte Homes Inc. — Pure Oil Middle East Inc. — al-Qa'ida — Qantas Airways Ltd. — Qatar — Qatar Fuel Additives Co. — Qatar Liquefied Gas Co. Ltd. (Qatargas) — The Qatar General Petroleum Corp. (QGPC) — Qatar Vinyl Co. (QVC) — QatarGas Upstream — QBE Insurance Group Ltd. — QLogic Corp. — Quaker Oats Co. — QUALCOMM Inc. — Quest Diagnostics Inc. — Qwest Communications Intl. Inc. — RadioShack Corp. — Rainforest Action Network — Rainforest Alliance — Rajneeshee — Ralcorp Holdings Inc. — RAND Corp. — Ras Laffan LNG Co. Ltd. (RasGas) — Rassemblement congolais pour la Democratie (RCD) — Raytheon Co. — Real Irish Republican Army (IRA) — Reckitt Benckiser — Recontra

380 — Recontras — Red Army Faction (RAF) — Red Brigades (BR) — Red Hand Defenders (RHD) — Reed Elsevier NV — Regions Financial Corp. — Renault — The Renco Group Inc. — The Rene Dubos Center for Human Environments Inc. — Rentokil Initial — Repsol YPF — Republic Services Inc. — Resistencia Nacional Mocambicana (RENAMO) — ResourceAfrica — Reuters Group — Revolutionary Association of the Women of Afghanistan (RAWA) — Revolutionary Cells — Revolutionary Council of Nigeria (RCN) — Revolutionary Justice Organization — Revolutionary Left — Revolutionary Nuclei (RN) — Revolutionary Organization 17 November — Revolutionary Organization of Socialist Muslims — Revolutionary Organization of the Toilers of Kurdistan — Revolutionary People's Liberation Party/Front (DHKP/C) — Revolutionary People's Struggle (ELA) — Revolutionary Proletarian Initiative Nuclei (NIPR) — Revolutionary Struggle — Revolutionary United Front (RUF) — Riceland Foods Inc. — Rich Products Corp. — Ricoh Co. Ltd. — Rio Tinto — Rios Vivos — Riyadus-Salikhin Reconnaissance and Sabotage Battalion of Chechen Martyrs — Rocco Food Brands — Roche Holding Ltd. — Rockwell Automation Inc. — Rockwell Collins Inc. — Rodamco Europe — Rohm Corp. — Rohm and Haas Co. — Rolls-Royce — Romania — Royal Bank of Scotland Group — Royal Caribbean International — Royal Dutch/Shell Group of Companies — Royal Philips Electronics — Russel Sage Foundation — Russell Stover Candies Inc. — Russia — Russian Organized Crime (ROC) — Rwanda — Rwandan Liberation Army — RWE — Ryanair Holdings — SABMiller — Sabre Holdings Corp. — Sabreliner Corp. — Safe Motherhood — Safeco Insurance Cos. — Safeway Inc. — Saheed Khalsa Force — St. Helena — St. Kitts and Nevis — Saint Lucia — Saint-Pierre and Miquelon — St. Vincent and the Grenadines — Salafist Group for Call and Combat (GSPC) — Samoa — San Jacinto Petroleum Corp. — San Marino — Sanderson Farms Inc. — Sandvik Group — Sankyo Co. Ltd. — Sanofi-Synthelabo Inc. — Sanpaolo IMI — Sanyo Electric Co. Ltd. — São Tomé and Principe — SAP — Sara Lee Corp. — Saudi Arabia — Saudi Arabian Oil Co. (Saudi Aramco) — Saudi Aramco Mobil Refinery Co. Ltd. (SAMREF) — Saudi Basic Industries Corp. (SABIC) — Saudi Marketing and Refining Co.

(SAMAREC) — Saudi Petroleum International Inc. — Saudi Petroleum Overseas Ltd. — Saudi Refining Inc. — SBC Communications Inc. — Scandinavian Airlines System — Scana — Scania — Schering AG — Schering-Plough — Schlumberger Ltd. — Schneider Electric — Science Applications Intl. Corp. (SAIC) — Scottish and Southern Energy — Scottish Power — Seaboard Corp. — Seagate Technology LLC — Sealed Air Corp. — Sears, Roebuck and Co. — Seat Pagine Gialle — SECOM — Securitas — Seibu Railway — Sekisui House Ltd. — Sempra Energy — Sendero Luminoso (SL) — Seneca Foods Corp. — Senegal — Serb Volunteer Guard (SDG/SSJ) — Serbia and Montenegro — Serbian Radical Party (SRS) — Serono Group — 7-Eleven — Severn Trent — Seychelles — Shan Democratic Union — Sharp Electronics Corp. — Shell Gas BV — Shell Transport & Trading Co. — The Sherwin-Williams Co. — Shikoku Electric Power Co. Inc. — Shin-Etsu Chemical Co. Ltd. — Shining Path (SL) — Shionogi & Co. Ltd. — Shiseido Co. Ltd. — Shizuoka Bank Ltd. — Shora-e-Jehad — Siebel Systems Inc. — Siemens — Sierra Leone — Sigma-Aldrich Co. — Signal Oil and Gas Co. — Simon Property Group — Singapore — Singapore Airlines — Singapore Press Holdings Ltd. — Singapore Telecommunications (SingTel) — Sipah-e-Sahaba Pakistan (SSP) — Sisterhood Is Global Institute — Gray Wolves (Sivi Vukovi) — Skandinaviska Enskilda Banken — Skelly Oil Co. — Simbionese Liberation Army (SLA) — Slovakia — Slovenia — SMC — Smith & Nephew — Smith International Inc. — Smithfield Foods Inc. — Smiths Group — Smurfit-Stone Container Corp. — Snam Rete Gas — Social Watch — Sociedad Peruana de Derecho Ambiental (SPDA) — Societatea Ecologica BIOTICA — Société Générale — Socony — Sodexho Alliance — Softbank — Standard Oil Co. of Ohio (SOHIO) — Solidaridad Internacional — Solomon Islands — Soltek Pacific of San Diego — Solvay — Somalia — Sompo Japan Insurance Co. of America (SJA) — Sony Corp. — South Africa — South Georgia and the South Sandwich Islands — South Lebanon Army (SLA) — Southern Co. — Southern Natural Gas Co. — Southern Ocean — SouthTrust Corp. — Southwest Airlines Co. — Southwest Marine Inc. — Sovereign Bancorp — Spain — Special Purpose Islamic Regiment (SPIR) — Specialty Foods Corp. — Spratly Islands — Sprint Corp. —

Sprint Fon Group — Sprint PCS Group — Sri Lanka — SsangYong Motor Co. — Ssangyong Oil Refining Co. — St. George Bank Ltd. — Standard Chartered Bank — Standard Oil of Indiana — Stanford University — Staples Inc. — Starbucks Corp. — Starwood Hotels & Resorts Worldwide Inc. — State Street Corp. — Statoil — Stewart & Stevenson Services Inc. — Stiftung Europaisches Naturerbe — STMicroelectronics — Stora Enso — Stryker Corp. — Students of the Engineer — Students of Ayyash — Sudan — Sudan People's Liberation Army (SPLA) — Sudan People's Liberation Movement (SPLM) — Suez — Suiza Foods Corp. — Sumitomo Chemical Co. Ltd. — Sumitomo Corp. — Sumitomo Electric Industries Ltd. — Sumitomo Mitsui Financial Group Inc. — Sumitomo Trust & Banking Co. Ltd. — Sun Hung Kai Properties Ltd. — Sun Life Financial Services of Canada — Sun Microsystems Inc. — Suncor Energy Inc. — Suncorp-Metway Ltd. — SunGard Data Systems Inc. — Sunkist Growers Inc. — Sunray DX Oil Co. — Sunray Mid-Continent Oil Co. — SUNS South-North Development Monitor — SunTrust Banks Inc. — Superior Oil Co. Inc. — Supreme Assembly of the Islamic Revolution in Iraq (SAIRI) — Supreme Council for Islamic Revolution in Iraq (SCIRI) — Suriname — Survival International — Suzuki Motor Corp. — Svalbard — Svenska Cellulosa Aktiebolaget — Svenska Handels-banken — Sverdrup Corp. — Swatch Group — Swaziland, the Kingdom of — Sweden — Swire Pacific Ltd. — Swiss Re — Swisscom Group — Switzerland — Symantec Corp. — Syngenta — Synopsys Inc. — Synovus Financial Corp. — Synthes-Stratec — Syria — Sysco Corp. — T. Rowe Price Group — Taisho Pharmaceutical Co. Ltd. — Taiwan — Tajikistan — Takeda Chemical Industries Ltd. — Takefuji Corp. — Talaa' al-Fateh — Taliban — Talisman Energy Inc. — Tanzania — Target Brands Inc. — Tata Energy Research Institute (TERI) — Technical Centre for Agricultural and Rural Cooperation (CTA) — Tele-X — Telecom New Zealand Group — Telecom Italia Mobile (TIM) — Teledyne Technologies Inc. — Telefónica — Telefónica Móviles — Telekom Austria — Telenor — Télévision Française (TF) — TeliaSonera — Telstra — TELUS — Tenet Healthcare Corp. — Terra Lliure (TL) — Terra Networks — Territorial Anti-Imperialist Nucleus — Tesco — Texas Instruments Inc. — Textron Inc. — Thailand —

Thales Group — Thiokol Corp. — 3rd October Organization — Third
World Network (TWN) — Thomson Corp. — 3M — ThyssenKrupp —
Tibetan Center for Human Rights and Democracy (TCHRD) —
Tidewater Oil & Gas Co. — Tiffany & Co. — TJX Cos. — Togo (The
Togolese Republic) — Tohoku Electric Power Co. Inc. — Tokelau —
Tokyo Electric Power Co. (TEPCO) — Tokyo Electron Ltd. (TEL) —
Tokyo Gas Co. Ltd. — TonenGeneral Sekiyu — Tonga, the Kingdom
of — T-Online International — Toppan Printing Co. Ltd. —
Torchmark Corp. — Toronto Dominion Bank Financial Group —
Toshiba Corp. — Tostem Inax Holding Corp. — Total — Total
Peripherals Group (TPG) — Total System Services Inc. — Toyota
Industries Corp. — Toyota Motor Corp. — Tracor Inc. — Transatlantic
Holdings Inc. — Transocean Inc. — Travelers Property Casualty — Tri
Valley Growers Inc. — Triarc Cos. Inc. — Trinidad and Tobago —
TriWest Healthcare Alliance Co. — Tromelin Island — Tropenbos
International (TBI) — TRW Inc. — Tunisia — The Tunisian
Combatant Group — Tupac Amaru Revolutionary Movement
(MRTA) — Tupac Katari Guerrilla Army (EGTK) — Turkey —
Turkish Islamic Jihad — Turkish People's Liberation Army —
Turkmenistan — Turks and Caicos Islands — Tuvalu — TXU Corp. —
Tyco International Ltd. — Tyson Foods Inc. — UBS — UFJ Holdings
— Uganda — Uganda National Rescue Front (UNRF) — Uganda
National Rescue Front II (UNRFII) — Uganda Salvation Front/Army
— Uighur Militants — Ukraine — Ulster Defence Association (UDA)
— Ulster Freedom Fighters (UFF) — Ulster Volunteer Force (UVF) —
Ultramar Ltd. — UNED Forum — União Democrática Timorense
(UDT) — UNICOR — UniCredito Italiano Bank — Unilever
Bestfoods — Union des forces vives pour la libération et la democra-
tie en RDC-Zaire (UFLD) — Unión Fenosa Group — Union Nacional
por la Independencee Totale Do Angola (UNITA) — Union Nationale
de la Femme Tunisienne (UNFT) — Union Oil Co. — Union Pacific
Corp. — Union Planters Bank — Union pour la libération nationale
(ULINA) — UnionBanCal Corp. — Unisys — Unit for Sustainable
Develop-ment and Environment — United Arab Emirates — United
Company of Jihad — United Concordia Cos. Inc. (UCCI) — United
Jihad Council — United Kingdom — United Liberation Front of

Assam (ULFA) — United Nations — United Overseas Bank — United Parcel Service of America Inc. (UPS) — United Self-Defense Forces/Group of Colombia (AUC) — United States — United Technologies Corp. — United Utilities — United Wa State Army (UWSA) — UnitedHealth Group — Universities Research Association Inc. — University of California — University of Chicago — University of Texas — Univision Communications Inc. — Unocal Corp. — UnumProvident Corp. — UPM-Kymmene Finland — Uruguay — Utz Quality Foods Inc. — Uzbekistan — Väestöliitto — Valero Energy Corp. — Vanguards of Conquest — VanStar Corp. — Vanuatu — Varian Medical Systems Inc. — Vatican City (Holy See) — Venezuela — Veolia Environnement — VeriSign Inc. — VERITAS Software — Verizon Communications — VF Corp. — Viacom Inc. — Vietnam — Vigorous Burmese Student Warriors — Virgin Islands — Virtual Academy for the Semi-Arid Tropics (VASAT) — Vivendi Universal — VNU — Vodafone Group — Vodafone-Panafon — Volkswagen — Volvo Group — Vornado Realty Trust — VSE Corp. — Vulcan Materials Co. — W.W. Grainger Inc. — Wachovia Corp. — Wake Island — Walgreens Co. — Wallis and Futuna — Wal-Mart Stores — Walt Disney Co. — Wanadoo — Wang Laboratories Inc. — Warner-Lambert Co. — Washington Mutual Inc. — The Washington Post — Waste Management Inc. — Watch Indonesia! — Water Development Federation (WDF) — Water Supply and Sanitation Collaborative Council (WSSCC) — Waters Corp. — Watson Pharmaceuticals Inc. — Weather Underground Organization (WUO) — Weatherford International Ltd. — Weathermen — Weight Watchers International Inc. — Welch Food Inc. — Wella Group — WellPoint Health Networks Inc. — Wells Fargo & Co. — Wesfarmers Ltd. — West Nile Bank Front (WNBF) — Western Sahara — Westfield Holdings Ltd. — Westfield Trust — Westinghouse Electric Corp. — Westpac Banking Corp. — Westwood One Inc. — Weyerhaeuser — The Wharf (Holdings) Ltd. — Whirlpool Corp. — WIDE (Network Women in Development Europe) — Wildlife and Environment Society of South Africa (WESSA) — Willis Group Holdings Ltd. — Wintershall — Wm. Morrison Supermarkets — Wolseley — Wolters Kluwer — WOMANKIND Worldwide — Women in Law and

Development in Africa (WiLDAF) — Women in Security, Conflict
Management and Peace (WISCOMP) — Women's Federation for
World Peace International (WFWPI) — Women's International
Coalition for Economic Justice (WICEJ) — Women's International
Democratic Federation (WIDF) — Women's International Zionist
Organization (WIZO) — Women's Learning Partnership — Women's
Peace Network (MADRE/WPN) — Women's World Summit
Foundation (WWSF) — WomenAction — Woodside Petroleum Ltd.
— Woolworths Ltd. — World Business Council for Sustainable
Development (WBCSD) — The World Commission on Dams (WCD)
— The World Conservation Union (IUCN) — World Federation of
Ukrainian Women's Organizations (WFUWO) — World March of
Women — World Neighbors — World Organisation Against Torture
(OMCT) — World Rainforest Movement (WRM) — World Resources
Institute (WRI) — World Tamil Association (WTA) — World Tamil
Movement (WTM) — World Watch Institute — World Young
Women's Christian Association (World YWCA) — Worldcorp Inc. —
WPP Group — The Wrigley Co. — Wyeth — Xcel Energy — Xerox
Corp. — Xilinx Inc. — XL Capital Ltd. — XTO Energy Inc. — Yahoo!
Inc. — Yamanouchi Pharmaceutical Co. Ltd. — Yamato Transport Co.
Ltd. — Yearbook of International Cooperation on Environment and
Development — Yemen — Yonge Nawe Environmental Action Group
— Yue Yuen Industrial Holdings Ltd. — Yugoslavia — Yum! Brands —
Zakum Development Co. — Zambia — Zapatista National Liberation
Army (EZLN) — Zimbabwe — Zimbabwe African National Union
(ZANU) — Zimbabwe Human Rights NGO Forum — Zimmer
Holdings Inc. — Zions Bancorporation — Zonta International —
Zurich Financial Services

iii: Lateox Dov

Lateox: late, latex, toxic

Dov: Heb.: bear

Dov: Assemblyman of 48th district, including
Borough Park, Dyker Heights, Kensington,
and parts of Flatbush

Dov: P's crush on a beautiful blond named Dov, unrequited
and painful

Recording Over

I might bask for a moment in the departed
and what's left,
when gone for a moment, and gone
for good. The quick traces
left in the falling
wake;
the bedded pause,
light up and fade of lexical access throws off false positives,
        for when subjects "recalled" 40 percent
        of the critical lures that had not, in fact,
        been presented, it was due to their
        being activated, or primed, by others
        related semantically, with rates
        of false recall at 55 percent. The genuine
        intrusive memories of the first group
        and the pseudomemories of the second
        are both experienced as involuntary,
        vivid, and emotionally evocative. That is,
        genuine memories and pseudomemories
        of trauma *feel* the same, but one is historically
        accurate and the other is not.
Carried the crates into the back, under the extended eaves,
each slat let in a broad channel of air
to cool the flies gently drawn across the table,
slowly spreading as if tiny air postulators
spinning in toward the moon,
a pile of moons—I mean the fruit,
fired in idealized shapes.
There are structures in the mind
beyond emotion, which is very hard to fake, beyond delight.
You are beaming beyond eros and the actual stuff,
mohair and camel hair,
that singed lamb smell, ephedrine dried,
        clearing space for another dream of 4-storey
        houses individually altered and augmented,
        arranged to individual tastes that foster
        passionate and loving elective affinities

via equitable proprietary shares
exchangeable transnationally and governed by 12-member
rotating boards that focus on common local
interests and have the option, as now,
of DVD players at Target for $44.97.
I said I would read "Stare into the Common
Joy" if I did this, and here, peering
through the poor circles of an invented scrip,
$5 co-payment. Filed
down to cart height,
sticking to the stamp,
bursting into code,
feeling for the lamp,
I cast aspersions toward complete kinesis,
but still lay prone to mastoid insult,
salinous and sodden. The air
makes clear the lost tenting space;
aestheticised passing out astonished
little helps, the fairest things
vanished into unclose
smiling air, rotting bosc.
Into every vacuum seethes someone
willing to make tiny, horrendous
orders, the flow itself
blotted lightly,
only, when un-
coagged, to thicken again at the first sign of movement,
as if to exhaust itself had been a posture,
an exceptional position it does not occupy,
                as with the installation of the 'interim' governments.
                Hamid Karzai, the interim Prime Minister of Afghanistan
                (which is not an American colony),
                with whom I have been compared physically
                at work as people have tried to come to terms
                with a decision made for them as citizens,
                was a top adviser to the El Segundo, California-based UNOCAL
                Corporation, which had been negotiating with the Taliban

to construct a natural gas pipeline from Turkmenistan
through western Afghanistan to Pakistan,
where I haven't been and can't go though relatively free.
Tosses thoughts
like incarnate tennis balls,
pompeiian
ash come
to life,
rushing up too much
too easily.
Porters
walking tragic,
shiny buttress flies,
mirrors under buses,
papers under flies,
   We trade speeches as the B61 blows by
   on Bedford. I stick the speakers
   on either side of the mic
   and cover the mass with a towel,
   losing the pans.

Salt Lake 2002

Toward the Chute. Phat air.

Self-imposed exigencies, a kind of false evolutionary pressure, snake down
consciousness and ruins of runs that jump the banks, corralling, veering
into box for a pop tart. Brain as Snoopy.

Youth, describe, say, authority. Every snowfall, it seems, expedites.
The windows worked, it all worked; not "technological"—
"toward liberation": the shiny tight suits are not uniforms.

Half-obscured by the hanging blanket, filth run down the sunken plumbing,
welded air passages vent involuntarily, put supervascular
crude extractionist, teleo-inevitable autonomy in play.

Intense polymer bonds. Red cheeks and the superhuman arm.
Fucking intense half-pipe.

Non-Potable

Piping in the non-potable, cutting holes in buildings.
When the tankers are scoured
the residue is brownish and gritty,
blasted out with steam, itself recouped under
pressure from the Navy Pier Desalinization Center,
designed by competition. The insides
of the tankers absolutely clear
when full, run on clean nukes.

I think "Monsanto" every time I take a shower
and get the greasy slick Asimov imagined for the moon.
I tell my screened children, images
projected from analyzation, about 20 minute
stints in the potable, pores like little gaping mouths.
Tanker's slick pontoon
at rest perpendicular to the former Yemen.
Every little cough a magnified annoyance.

Marshall Plan

The 'Japanese
street' actually
boils
over;

hundreds
of thousands
of civilian
spirits

walk
toward
Washington,
are

detained,
held;
a Shinto
ceremony

proves
ineffective;
Billy Graham
gets

access
nowhere,
nor does
Jesse;

Tikkun
forum scuttled
and
NPR...

Democratic Process as Feed Lot

The explosive energy within the cornfed cow not possible to contain in
        hypermarbling or digestive fortitude—
four of five stomachs fail, even when shot up with cortisone, which reaches
        right to the joints, radiating,
when ingested, from infixed knuckles and knees rarely brought to full
        extension, but the corn's energy

overpowers, like the sun's by the flat Sound, burning head tops and elbows
        without distinction.

The Ways that Windows Fit into [Casements]

The tightness of the seal deceptive, since never absolute, yet, like antibacterial
        soaps, works toward assuagement,

blown through the general appetite that ends in sponsored deliberation. We
        must recreate the complex of feeling that drove...

Take another secret tablet to take it further: four times six is twenty-four, six
        times eight is forty eight, Kennedy caravan is sixty three,

Eight times twelve is 1996. He is six feet five, prostrate on your table. He
        stuck it on his head and he cried.

Leader

You won't read it when I to write to you, nor see me
except within sanctioned spaces of agreement,
much as representation drowns out its patrons
in the generalized din of trying to park.

When you refused to get up and walk your dog
(the mucus ran dark) and I couldn't get the elevator
to come, "Sundance" percolated unbearably,
forcing us into the stairwell and down the 17

double height flights to the sandy expanse, done
up in ballfield chainlink. As she relieved
herself I thought of you asleep, easily rising
to piss when it suited you, the alarm tuned to KTU

yet ineffectual, light.
When I later confronted you with your take-out
in my navy windbreaker with blue poly fur
(false ruff), you seemed embarrassed,

and I could imagine a kind of vindication
but felt...*nothing*. Level of hydration
turns out to be a class marker,
bare neck a vulnerability.

Lateox Dov (Elastic Bear)

I think the money you have to spend on a thing to love
is destroyed by anaphylaxis.

I couldn't see you because of the *glair*, differentiated.

  "Friends, when it's ready,
I want that red heifer, Kampf,
brought directly to my office";
 you
   be the judge, climb
      a monticule
          that suggests
    dictionary work,
      endlessly replay
       the initial assent,
     September 28, 2000
      —a 'catastrophe',
     especially as
     the work,
   which continues
    to involve the sawing down
      of large boulders from the Second Temple
   period with the help of a giant electric saw
      and the draining of cistern #5,
    was going smoothly.

  Liberalism an easily led spotted calf
coming to consciousness,
  gaining all four legs,
  coated, like a finger protector,
 for quicker donning
with an eye
  to the maternal tongue.
Unstated threats wash through the air
    like unsalted nuts, unformed cursive,
   numerous possible unrealized consequences,
     or simple expressions of systemic weakness
  (another word rendered as 'struggle'),
  as the bear lies down in the stall, stretching
  its entire bulk over the defiant youth.

Deposition

You feel sorry for me because I never made aliyah (www.aliyah.org).
I watch you, a band apart, pack up and move out of Boro Park
because the Syrian Jews aren't "frum."
But if the Kaiser had won, the Ottoman Empire might still exist,
might be empire,
might

Reaction shots faster than bionics
keep collaborative brain space from developing,
being beamed back to earth, while segmented units, cut outs,
form the axes of a smashed green fence, supply-side
effervescent cuspid, the old ticker.
Tens of thousands of clicks separate us from

                    Clamp

                                        lie.

            3 positions further.

                                Lie.

    Quartet.

Visitors

Fleet week. Beef protection:
men + women and me the same.

Big bags of trash glossy like cows
lain in the lot by the pier stink of fry.

Fog really *like*
dry ice.

Directions cheerfully given
before compaction.

The Magic Flute

A mental economy in which aid-work lessens
the contradictions and maintains painful international relationships:
sit at desk and get paid; checks to Doctors Without Borders
undercut by self-flex momentita which sends you out
into *la terre de la pipe*, hot,
totally flat at the abs, broken for scrap.
"Nets and Bubbles" depict floating white
glutinous balls in dark tea on a dark ground.
Will the waterproof coating on my jacket
come off on my hands and get onto my dick
when I take a break? By the time you've perfected
your affect, learned the range of circumstances
you're likely to encounter and what some
effective responses and carriages are,
you'll be in a home, watching tiny televised people
in fields and factories on PBS before the performance.

Contract Law

If every exchange is negotiated with the presumption of bad faith,
the only possible way to come away with even a piece of what you
want is to propose basic terms that you have no intention of fulfilling,
while feeling around for what givens on the other side can be seized
and services extracted without further harm to you, though the tenets
of the system be destroyed. Thus one does real business with family,
from whom there is no extraction, and on whom survival often depends,
so is neo-sacralized, while any outside encounter provides opportunities
for real advancement on terms that can be as fresh as one's devising,
with no disturbance to the interior life. This is a failure of contract law,
a primary means of exclusion, and an aspect of state failure in general,
along with environmental depredation, disputes over birth rates,
and thousands of incalculable daily forms of threat and coercion
culminating in violent death that achieves sporadic documentation.

Leviathan

The paper ring is slightly absorptive,
and I don't want my leg-skin to have to tax
its resources resisting organisms after rising.

I want that energy
pushed back
into other endeavors.

Lake Effect

Oar lock. Limitations on the paddle.
Motion redirected. Tiny Arnold.

Latkes. Gloves. Grover.

Eensy-weensy tip
nock tup.

Leviathan

Images of Artificial Man.

The language of the force
that will occupy the space.

My Twin

The wig looked monstrous—one could see
the small pricks in the back
where the synthetic auburn tendrils toward
the pink nape case the brain stem
housing involuntary vital functions, breathing,
heartbeat, thanatos.

The sound for the voice box has to be fantastic,
the playback perfect—you have to have
a place to physically put the past
to move it.

The East River

We're still reading Majakovskii through O'Hara.

Waving
from U Thant Island
at the massed diplomats.

We don't know what was said.

Sleep and Poetry

A helicopter;
a hectare over the water.

For a change, the helicopter
is here, reflected dread not relevant,

relief embarrassing, handed thickly
across like an involuntary sandbag of sound,

the dark hull heavy,
on credit;

orange light on blues and bricks and isolated
sounds in the wake.

Elsewhere, they entered the area with bulldozers
and set up camp directly over the aquifer,

making actual measure, and reporting immediately
instead of secondarily registering via sought traces

in larger-scale effects the drawn lines of another
test of relations in violent seizure.

We say whatever we feel;
they do whatever they want.

Poetry as a struggle
for representative agency.

Poetry as a struggle
for psychological liberty,

which has a material basis,
heavily used though in truth

not badly degraded,
if in fact.

A substitute,
like religion,

but despite
defaillancy,

retains
capacity,

deathless
excess,

space
unremarked.

Science, like poetry, can enable incredible violence,
pointed carelessly or aimed intentionally;

Science never an absolute political tool
unless materialized;

Religion never an absolute political tool unless moralized,
yet capable of carrying great forgiveness.

Since the issues are pressing,
there is an undeniable journalistic element,

and since there has been
plenty of straight reporting,

and internal monographization
for those whose bodies are actually involved,

the relative aestheticization,
and, *mutatis mutandis*,

the appropriation
of these issues may be permissible.

Permission itself implies a body
that can grant it, and that is always

people, and one is people, even if codifying
relationships to the land that, like religion,

seem sacred but have been
wired in by time and habit.

There's a method for remaking relations; it is called science,
and its materialist trajectory insulates it,

relatively, from the critique of aestheticization,
though some would argue that the organization

and analysis of data—the transformation
of the land and the lives of people into data—is a movement similar

to the synthetic appropriation of poetry,
the force that is used to put something

in a poem, since it does not come by itself, regardless of the excuse—
the social role played by the usual agents embodying

the terms of a metaphor at the time of its construction, but regardless
taking dictation. After math, everything.

Law does not seem as objective as science.
The imagination is part of the real material conditions of one's life.

iv: Model States

What we must chiefly bear in mind, then, is that physical society in time must never for a moment cease to exist while moral society as an idea is in the process of being formed; that for the sake of man's moral dignity his actual existence must never be jeopardized. When the craftsman has a timepiece to repair, he can let its wheels run down; but the living clockwork of the State must be repaired while it is still striking, and it is a question of changing the revolving wheel while it still revolves.

—Schiller, Third Letter on the
  Aesthetic Education of Humanity

And when some other minion said
stop! can't it all stop
for a moment?
that was high comedy
idealist tragedy

And now he's waiting for the same
time
as me

—Rodrigo Toscano, "Future Perfect"

Consciousness
combs with the sterile
shalelike concentric accumulation of remainder.
A light in already clear
waters, as advancement a median of the ever ready
tears in nine light
unanswered change, and brings dissolution.
The cemetery wheel of citizenship,
a theory of chance will not change.

—David Micah Greenberg, "Common Will"

Although no one has succeeded in teleporting so much as a single sub-atomic particle, some have managed to teleport the quantum states those particles are in. These states describe the exact characteristics of a particle, so in theory a body could be reconstructed particle by particle if enough quantum states were teleported.

—*The Economist* (June 19, 2004)

EVERY generation has apocalyptic visions, can't imagine its continuance, as in Rivette's *Paris nous appartient* (1960), where the exiled American communist journalist, experimenting with Art Brut in his SRO, warns Anne of converging super-militarized oligarchical death waves.

My apartment, which you'll recall from last time, is bathed in the sounds of a Red Bull event by the river, men and women amplified, shouting and generating excitement that somehow gets shunted into product, religious techniques, walking back and forth wireless.

A small amount of movement or sound has come to signify a mouse, a rebuke to systems of control by which people might be stamped out, round like a nickel and grey, with tails trailing and eyes bulging brown.

Citizens shouted very differently among their own remnants and ruins, Roman and otherwise, on 2/15/03, in the largest mass event and first global manifestation, against war or anything else, on record, detourning totalizing yelling into group demand, stamping the little silver cans into a huge reflective shield and straining to articulate what should follow, fighting enervation with dissolved caffeine and sucrose.

The scale of the problem causes fatigue because people create meaning in clan-sized groups, and Steve says there's a study that says one can only love 200 in a life, which seems to be a kind of parameter for the processing of affiliation, a limit which not coincidentally seems to underlie clans and anarchism, though my beliefs run to the bureaucratic materialism that underlies communism, so that it is at that scale, talking to friends, and with that result, a kind of communism, that I have found myself able to articulate a politics, one that proceeds from the scale of my social relations, rather than a totality.

If power, or the means for making and instantiating judgements, is changed in scale by relations that form by agreement, force, or ambient internalization, and if every articulation proposes, produces, or reifies sets of relations, then the distribution of power touches every articulation, since every articulation proposes relations, which form states.

The contradictions produced by power are shared, and their articulation, by poets and others, is a real, if unwanted, function within society, as is the modeling, in poems and other media, of other possible modes of power, as on Saturdays on Rain's tiny dancefloor on N 5 Street in Williamsburg, where I was first brought by poets, and where the men of the neighborhood admit me to a space of mutual movement that subsumes in an explicit manner never approached on the street, where I adjust my walk.

Power, an inevitable product of relations, necessarily alters bodies, often damaging, even if invisio-neuronally, or actually destroying them, as when conceptions of what is required for affiliation differ or get distorted when brought into proximity and enforced.

The mechanics by which power travels and changes scale, through agreement, force, or ambient internalization, is called politics, yet politics does not address bodies as such, except as instantiations of constructs in which power collects or doesn't, categories that can have a directly physical extension, like 'food', or a purely narrative function, like 'justice'.

Narrative is a set of proposed links among artificially segmented perceptions; narration is the act of proposing such links.

For power, shifts correlate to alterations in relations, which are physical, and can be augmented or protected by gloves, cars, guns, neighborhoods, tractors, planes, lending rates, coats, and computers, all of which change the scale of power, and in politics, shifts occur among sets of categories and catchments, also physical, casting shadows on never-fully-discrete bodies, and standing for them in the sense that it is to categories and catchments, or what get called subjects, rather than to bodies, that judgements are ascribed.

In film and fiction, such subjects, multi-faceted categories through which social relations, and thus power, run, are called characters, and turning people into characters is what makes non-novel readers so squeamish about fiction, since doing so, reducing people to sets of attributes, is a kind commodification, or at a least reification, one that mimics the market system that spawned fiction in the 18th century and with which, necessary changes having been made, we are familiar today.

Imagining commodification to be a result of market logic gets it backward, since turning people into products is a major part of sexual selection, a process regulated by mores and other constraints through which people are treated as acquirable wholes that can be broken down into particular attributes, desireable or undesireable, that are centered on images of fitness and out of which market logic falls, with shopping being a relation in which the 'partner' doesn't talk back or experience transference.

Turning people into characters is an amazingly effective political tool, since characters, like some commodities, do not suffer, die or react in real time, and are constructed for performances within narrow bandwidths that are very restricted when compared with the actual conditions most people face, but that are alike enough that the reduction is possible, since to resist such reductions requires more energy than to acquiesce.

Although characters, unlike horses and people, cannot respond to an idea that takes the form of force, such as a lash against a coach-and-six that carries the message 'go', it is as characters that politics prepares people for power, even when attacking one's material extension in space and attempting to reduce one to it. Death as message or story. Let's roll.

Rabbits, who have brains and bodies, are of course extraordinary, and their fierce rabbity love, while occasionally seeming aloof or unintelligible, is in fact one of the main model states, but rather than separating species, splitting characters from people draws materialism from humanism, so that discrete

fixed code units definable by parts can be replaced with
floating, dynamic points of contact for myriad forces never
fully visible or possible to specify but which can, with mutu-
al labor, sustain themselves, remain buoyant, partially self-
representational constructs with material bases, reducible by
violence to bodies, yet capable of producing excesses like
imagination.

• •

MY belief in the absolute material bases for staging such
positions, fictional or otherwise, is what forces me to think
about politics, along with a desire for affiliation without
reduction.

Art, or situations of partially suspended disbelief, of fore-
grounding, of heightening or intentional flattening, of pro-
tected description and inflated proposition, is a locus, in any
society at any scale, for staging relations as a kind of model.

By mutual agreements that do not differ from those of regu-
lar interactions, art proposes, rather than fully instantiates,
sets of relations, raising, and attempting temporarily to
appear to frame, the relations it produces, held like eye
contact.

Interactions around art, when they work, produce sensations
that require high levels of processing, so they tend to happen
in relatively protected spaces, never absolute or guaranteed,
analogous to airport cottages at Dayton or spartan dachas
outside of Reykjavík.

Deliberation requires a provisional affiliation, in the sense
of involuntarily imagining the consequences of sets of terms
and the relations they propose, which makes deliberation
disturbing, because affiliation can never be fully provisional,
which is what lies behind objections to images of violence,
which is why Spielberg claims to employ them only within

highly motivated meaning structures, preferring models of exchange based on art, as at the climax of *Close Encounters of the Third Kind* (1977), when a French disco scientist and an enormous extraplanetary craft undertake a musical rondo under the auspices of a finally indulgent U.S. military, which holds fire while a highly amplified, visually interpreted five tone sequence is put forth, and is tentatively and then forcefully taken up by the hovering vessel, which goes on to offer fantastical variations upon it at speeds that only computers and geniuses at the site can process, finally allowing a large number of MIAs to be disgorged from the hull without incident, along with a young blond boy who is the focus of the movie's driving mother love, counterpoint to Dreyfus's signature lone-male sublimations, followed by the letdown of the anthropomorphic, infantilized aliens.

Ascribing decisions to character is an act of judgement, and such acts are what make writing political, since judgement creates relations, and ascription is a kind of writing.

Aesthetic experience, or pleasure in sharing in proposing relations, art, can take place independently of explicit judgement, but is itself a form of affiliation, which has in the past led to critiques of the very 'absorption' that is necessary for many of its forms. Truffault plays the scientist.

Because relations are always material and judgement is always affiliation, in proposing sets of relations, any work that fails to examine the material bases on which it is itself predicated, at whatever level, risks contributing to its own misrecognition, and being appropriated to perpetuate myths of baseless relations and consequenceless judgement unbounded by materiality or affiliation, resulting in contradictions, a problem alternately dramatized and parodied in Chabrol's *Les Biches* (1968), where Jacqueline Sassard, intentionally young, striking and self-possessed in a manner that seems somehow greater, because incorporating reactionary classicism, than the impending *soixante-huitards*, produces, when asked her name by mid-30s shiny socialite Stephane Audran, a contemptuous, clearly enunciated «je m'appelle 'Why'», the English word

doubly empty, which delights Audran's character, who negoti-
ates with and appropriates Sassard's Why, providing access to
wealth and companionship that, when discontinued, eventually
lead to her own character's death.

• •

FOR the formalist, affiliation is a kind of death, the death of
doubt, agency, and possibility, with the exception of affiliation
with method, taken as a means for a kind of critique of
fantasies of transcendent maximalist infinitude.

By imposing rules and proposing relations along strictly mate-
rial lines, formalisms can analogize the limits imposed by
resources and belief systems, tacit and explicit, and surround,
alter or reorder their material instantiations, revealing their
provisionality, releasing joy from obligation and projected per-
petuity through a 'count your shit' recursion, which ironically
reveals the infinite in combination.

Formalism can thus work against a default or dominant that
presents itself as eternal and inviolable, and can function as an
indirect critique of entrenched sets of relations, by demonstrat-
ing parallel and even random position-takings and sets of rela-
tions as potentially equally meaningful and derived from simi-
lar limits.

Method produces an oppositional position of its own, struc-
tured play, that when taken as a model form of exchange can
change relations, but that when received as a product, confines
its effects to that of politico-aesthetic 'pressure valve', or means
of discharging the energy produced by contradictions so that
they might remain in place, a role provided for in most domi-
nant sets of relations, as when Zola writes, in *Germinal* (1885),
and elsewhere, of the effects of coffee and alcohol on workers.
Such contradictions, which most journalists ignore, are inher-
ent in conventional affiliations, and, when examined closely,
often produce apathy and fatigue, at least partially due to the
scales, far beyond the scope of character, at which they operate.

Since it's predicated on finitude, capitalism couldn't work if people didn't die.

Like science, which proceeds, theoretically, out of passionate materialist disinterest, but which, in actual practice, is almost wholly market-driven, maintaining contradictions is a business that produces its own class, one with which I identify, partly out a desire to master shifting social codes as a means of nonfamilial power, being beyond the house with the attorneys who formalize the language of exchange, the academics who undergird it, the journalists who naturalize it, the novelists who fetishize it, and the satirists who ironize it.

What is often meant by 'freedom' is the possibility of the acquisition of such codes, which, like other material acquisitions, become more expensive the more associated they are with power. 'Cool' is the attempt to recapture freedom by explicitly rejecting this dynamic, but its cooptation, and the anticipation of its cooptation, drive the provisionality and disposability of the codes and materials cool itself takes up, which also happens to artistic communities.

Artists invited me to join Friendster repeatedly, and I tried to turn the invitations to affiliation toward small actions of 5 or 15, but everyone with whom I spoke projected a need for definitions and justifications to release them from fatigue, which I saw as a defense against the perceived need for disaffiliation from power, and which I could not produce on the phone or in a bar.

Such projections are imbricated within the discourse of 'time', whereby one is consumed by work or attachment, and cannot imagine undertaking further action and self-representation, particularly in 'public', which implies submitting one's actions to large-scale collective judgement.

Most attempts to operate 'outside' of that judgement are represented as criminal, as in *Gun Crazy* (1949), where the lovers, on recognizing one another's interlocking needs, skillsets, self-presentations and physicalities, and, in attempting to manifest them fully and in concert, discover them to be unsustainable at the highest levels without constant infusions of money, triggering, beyond need for shelter and sustenance, feelings of rage and neglect that spill over into escalations of the types of 'jobs' they do, including killing those who seem to judge their acts, eventually leading to an escalation in the scale of pursuit that leads to their being cornered, or isolated without adaquate resources or means of further travel, and locked into an inarticulate choice between imprisonment or death.

• •

ALL characters need names so that decisions and values can be ascribed to them, and so do projections with which multiples might affiliate, like teams, an extension of subjectivity to partial intersubjectivity that allows one to possibly absorb violence in the belief that it will not arrive at a scale large enough to destroy the group. Stonewall was a riot.

The mass proposition of changes in specific sets of relations, protest, has been underminded by state agencies and corporations, aggregate characters granted rights of property and speech, that have developed practical tactics for preventing the scale of actions from reaching a tipping point or for making it look that way.

The fatigue gets overcome by 'extraordinary' events, like a war or a fraudulent election, but it does not seem to get overcome in the quotidian by people who feel secure but only provisionally so. Skinnerian partial reinforcement of the lack of guaranteed employment blocks the impulse toward resistance and advocacy by putting beliefs about what constitutes 'good' work, artistic or otherwise, as well as 'well spent' time, into conflict with resistance, which makes the idea of trying to put one's body someplace in a resisting or canvassing posture carry a high degree of fear, and makes it seem as if a legimating structure for doing so, let alone one that directly and coherently reflects one's beliefs, is impossible to construct.

The articulation of contradiction can cause catharsis and abreaction, the power of which can cause dis- and re-affiliation, a threat to forms of power.

Because forms get fetishized, they change, seeking fresh access to the energy that inheres in contradictions, so that at one point, when further shifts seemed impossible, the 'dematerialization' of the art object was attempted, meaning there was an agreement among artists and others to treat encounters, procedures, and acts of documentation as art, difficult to conserve.

Jauss's restatement of beauty (1977), "the form in which aesthetic experience presents itself," forces one to talk about specific instances and encounters, and encodes the impossibility of fully generalizing about form.

● ●

PARTIALLY because disaffiation is a kind of death, Fanon advocated violence as a means to catharsis and abreaction, which are sometimes produced by the destruction of bodies, and are real material resources, even if invisio-neuronal. Yet the trauma produced in survivors of violence, including those that inflict it, negates any momentary cathartic benefit, because the longterm consequences of violence include a tendency to replicate injury, perpetuating a 'cycle' that acquires narrative justifications as necessary. Fanon's own "Colonial War and Mental Disorders" (1961) can be read as registering instances of such replication, grounded in specific acts arising from internalized conditions of domination and oppression, while Semezdin Mehmedinovic's *Sarajevo Blues* (1998) records instances of paramilitary beheadings within a non-colonial city that the perpetrators justify through citations of acts of violence from prior centuries.

Representations of violence often take the form of entertainment, which can be a tool of control as well as a form of discursive preparation, which most killings require, and which usually reduces to a single character-trait:

"Someone who is threatening my life or that of someone I love" as most primal and most often given to actual soldiers, though video simulation and gaming also seem to suffice— Hollywood death

"Someone who is in league with a force that is exploiting and destroying us, and that will not recognize our condition"— Maoist death

"Someone who is a barrier or threat to my expansion, and that is impeding my extracting the full possible benefit from a situation"—capitalist death

"Someone who is staining our representation of the ideal, or the all, and our ways of relating to it"—religious death

Agency, or decisions acted upon with resultant chains of consequence, desired or undesired, produces contradictions that manifest as fatigue, in the sense of feeling unequal to circumstance, or as boredom, in the sense of feeling that all outcomes can be anticipated, or as frustration, in the sense of wanting cathartic resolution, which can be turned inward via self-abnegation.

Most of the suicides I have imagined have been passive: addressing the back of my head, in 1991, to the parking lot window of a first floor apartment in Providence so that bullets, whose trajectory would be perhaps a 20-degree-angle from the blacktop, fired by no one in particular, might pass between the burglar bars and into the cerebellum and stem, the old breathing brain, making little holes just at the top of the collar of the robe; or falling from an extremely fast-moving car and skidding slowly and painlessly, because blacking out, to a stop; or the gun fantasy of putting a fake plastic Uzi in my yellow vinyl shoulderbag and taking the 4 or 5 train to Wall Street, where I walk up to the barracades around the

Exchange, take out the gun and wave it in circles over my head, drawing a rain of extremely accurate, high-powered fire; but just now I became active, and could imagine exerting enough force on the tongue of my belt so that it would puncture the point just where the ribs part, making a kind of lower stoma, and pulling up for a tiny blunt evisceration.

Because I have imagined my own death through narcissistic fantasy, trying to imagine the deaths of others, as when reading the *New York Times*, feels compromised by that same narcissism: being slowly killed by silicosis in a rural Chinese factory that cuts fake gems; disappeared and tortured to death in Colómbia for making a neutral remark outside of Calí that gets me onto the list of one or another paramilitary *limpieza* faction; recruited as a soldier at age 10 and subsequently being decapitated in the Great Lakes region of Africa; raped and strangled in Gujarat in order to defile my religion as carried by my gendered body; shot in the face by a fearful cop in Harlem who has mistakenly invaded my home; bleeding to death after being suddenly shot with an automatic weapon while lined up at a coffee stand in Hebron; slashed in the throat in Pakistan after being forced to proclaim my religious affiliation and that of my kin; suffocating after being thrown down a well in any number of places because of gender-based resource allocation; or being killed in Kuwait by noncombat weapons discharge while mobilizing for deployment.

Yet because the surface conditions of 'my life' depend of sets of relations that produce those conditions, the attempt to imagine and render them must inform any work that proceeds from it, to the point that, in imagining extreme forms of my own subjugation, I fantasize that in nuclear death the brain is fast enough to complete, before vaporization, the full-replay that some have reported, since a 'good death' requires preparation, and while the duration of the flashbacks is reportedly long, the time elapsed, apparently, is not.

● ●

FANON wrote in French, and French continues, in areas to which it was forcibly brought, to be taken up in exigency and desire as well as disgust and repudiation, to produce economic effects for anyone whom it subsumes or engages, and to retain, like any language, natural or artificial, accumulative traces, some of which, for French, specifically remain from when it was taken up, some sixty years after France took Algeria, as Bergson's phenomenological instrument of *durée*, or duration, if not of time.

Time and duration depend on scale, in the sense that the sets of relations that produce them, gravitational and otherwise, are perceived as relatively stable and inviolate, though actually localized and in flux.

Time now dominates perception to the point that people take drugs to restore duration for short periods.

States, or dynamic, non-isolable arrangements of matter, succeed each other; time's incrementality marks, and thus represents, different states.

Time assigns values to successive states, which are forced by brains into three dimensions, with six tightly curled further planes, unimaginable but modelable, exerting their own pulls, which are manifest in the telepathy heightened by regular congress between electively affinitive persons, discrete units of what Foucault and Negri call biopower, which Haraway finds an absurd and flaccid reduction, despite Scarry's demonstrations of the innumerable ways in which that reduction is effected daily.

The more heightened such relations, the more character, in ecstasy, becomes what Hölderlin in *Hyperion* (1798) calls soul, and it assumes, in the throes of congress, classical proportions, meaning that the relation affords access to futher dimensions, as in grief.

To imagine all states, or to pick a state and then project or calculate its subsequent states from its trajectory, would be to travel in time, if the body be held stable.

If any one configuration could be isolated and held in stasis, it might form a 'stop' very unlike those for buses, where states alter during idling in the same manner as when in motion and the same internal fluctuations within the chassis continue, as in *Midnight Cowboy* (1969), where Ratso's death does not alter the body's course.

Nostalgia is the wish to reinstate collapsed relations. Fate is the coding of a determinate universe, in the sense of a course by which, given a certain configuration, energy will dissipate along with the chains of consequence surrounding agency. Free will is the manner in which senses maximize access to possible relational configurations, with a pitch toward destruction if unmet. There is a possible consciousness that might comprehend all possible states, and thus all time, but it is not necessary to imagine it.

Time and duration correlate to truth and fiction, both of which are required for love, a means of navigating the violence and involuntariness of attachment, as in *Late Sping* (1949), where the widower father of the character played by Setsuko Hara, a beautiful young woman who is on the cusp reaching an age that will make her a less desirable match, leads her to believe that he will remarry, so that she will shift her primary attachment from him to her suitor. Truth is dick shots on craigslist, or the petroleum element of vegetarian duck. Ethics is a system for weighing competing goods, and for assigning a value to relations, like shame.

Narrative is a set of proposed links among artificially segmented perceptions marked by time; narration is the act of proposing such links, even if untrue, in order to saturate duration.

Dialects of English use of the subjunctive progressive to mark the unreal, constantly revised present as never fully experienced, as in *Stalker* (1979), where a glass of milk's movement means either that superhuman powers are acquired through catastrophe, or that one moves a body without witness in belief.

I was sitting at home in these various states when the clock suddenly went out and the fridge stopped. "In a few moments, will be clear whether this was an electromagnetic pulse or a power failure." Long durée oddly calm, and then slowly lifted the phone. It worked.

v: At the Met

A supplementary twist is provided by the very end of the movie, when Neo magically stops the bad squidlike machines attacking the humans by merely raising his hand. How was he able to accomplish this in the "desert of the real," not within the Matrix where, of course, he can do wonders? Does this unexplained inconsistency indicate that "all there is is generated by the Matrix," that there is no ultimate reality? Although such a postmodern temptation—the easy way out of ontological confusion—is to be rejected, there is a correct insight in this complication of the simple and straight division between the "real reality" and the Matrix-generated universe. Even if the struggle takes place in the "real reality," the key fight is to be won in the Matrix, which is why the human rebels re-enter its virtual universe.

To put it in terms of the good old Marxist couple infrastructure/superstructure: One should take into account the irreducible duality of, on the one hand, the "objective" material socio-economic processes taking place in reality as well as, on the other hand, the politico-ideological process proper. What if the domain of politics is inherently "sterile," a theater of shadows, but nonetheless crucial in transforming reality? So, although economy is the real site and politics a theater of shadows, the main fight is to be fought in politics and ideology.

—Slavoj Zizek, "Ideology Reloaded"

When the entourage decided on Michael Moore's Fahrenheit 911, the rock star protested saying, "I don't want to see that, it's all propaganda." This sparked a prolonged political debate in front of the theater where Simmons claimed that Kid Rock said, "Russell, don't you understand, everything we got in this country, we got from fighting...I'd rather go to the bar across the street." He then refused to go into the theater with the others and said goodbye. A couple of hours later, Simmons returned to his parked car where a note was found on the windshield that read, "Vote Bush. Bush Rocks," allegedly written by Kid Rock.

—http://www.filmhobbit.com/forum/archive/topic/11600—1.html

Douglas and I went up to the Met yesterday afternoon - April 19, 2003 - I brought a sign - Alissa met us there - I stood w/ sign on the sidewalk by steps near the central set of railings that leads to the entrance - text:

::

Country built on plunder.

"Free" Markets DESTROY history.
        people and their arts

$lavery's legacy Unspoken and Unpaid.

Native
512 Nations Obliterated.

Who Stole <u>Iraq's Past</u>?

Whose is <u>Next</u>?

Enjoy the "Egyptian Wing."

::

Some encounters:

::

Well-heeled white senior couple - he "agrees absolutely" - she's furious, fixating on provenance of items in Japanese museums - they stay quite a while - Doug in long conversation with the guy - he, Egyptian-born Jewish - she, a Brit - married 56 years - "He was probably fighting age as Rommel crossed the Libyan border," Doug says later.

::

Af-Am kid on bicycle stops to read the sign. I say it's a response to the sackings, describe a little of what happened - nods.

::

Two young guys from India - one notes "There are more Egyptian artifacts here than anywhere except Egypt" - gets into v. long conversation with Doug, other guy not wanting to talk.

::

Elderly white guy with slight Euro accent - "That's what happens. War is hell."

::

Little crowds sort of form and dissipate of people reading - mostly not commenting but trying it out - talk to some, say it's a response to the looting, which U.S. force under Geneva convention was obliged to prevent - drawing links to earlier empires' plundering and, at v. least, enablement of the movement of such objects - objects landing here via robber-baron collectors - compromise resolution of provenances only begun in recent years - (had looked up Dendur - apparently Nasser gave it to the U.S. in 1965 - can't imagine)

Keep trying to focus on polit. consequences of this loss: on physical loss, on symbolic role it is likely to play, on how much it is congruent with this country's actual history - just rolling over things in the way of doing business and getting at resources -

Careful to point out that de Montebello and others in "museum community" desperately trying to mop up (partially no doubt b/c of the remaining shaky standing of much of what they hold) - two U.S. interior ministers have resigned - need to communicate that citizen- ry cares about loss of life and culture even if govt determined to destroy and remove and make it look like benign neglect -

Alissa's interviewing people and taking pictures - three museum guards seemingly on break or recon. very enthusiastic - all young males - one white, one mid east, one latino - then craggy white hip- ster-looking guy on bike - AQ later says he was an RTmark-er - many others.

::

Douglas later re: Dendur: "they build the aswan high damn...it was going to flood out this ancient valley filled (?) with antiquities - specifically the 'huge legs of stone' seen (?) & (or) reported by shelley in his poem...the reality is that the legs, unlike in the poem, are attached to the huge seated bodies of Ramsees the great....anyway, they had to move these to higher ground.

"the international community sent tons of money to pay for the movement in return for the $ and help, 'we' negotiated the 'removal' of some of the antiquities that were not going to be moved....so as the waters of the new lake nasar were licking at the base of the stones, the temple (having been hand picked by the prezident's wifey) was dismantled & trucked away. years later Jackie O' was known to refer it as 'my temple'. it was commissioned by Augustus.

"most of the above can be read on the walls of the museum when you go into the temple room itself.

"(i don't know when the exhibit opened, but i'm pretty sure it was not on view till the 70's)"

::

Older Ossie Davis-looking guy: "Are you crazy? You must be crazy."

::

Young South Asian woman - stylish, pageboy-like hair - asks if she can take my picture with the sign - "I'm going to take this back to Pakistan."

::

Cop tells me to keep moving. I say, I'm on the sidewalk. She says, it's the Met's sidewalk, and they don't condone political activity - I say, I'm just standing here, and there's no way they own the sidewalk - she says, they do, from 81st to 88th, I'm just informing you - I think, if I move around a little for a minute or two she's done her job, and we can do another round if necessary - I say "ok" - she drifts off - I move around a little - seems to work, though this I think would be a problem with more people in an organized thing - and there's no way they (Met) can actually have control of "their" sidewalk, is there? Granted land as part of Central Park?

Kid Rock-looking guy - small blue eyes - long, shiny thin mouse brown hair dyed appealingly and lightly blond - rangy guy, tall - very thin - maybe 30 - little mounds and white opaque calluses on his white outstretched hand - says -

You see this hand [visibly shaking]?
This is a working man's hand.
Hands like this built this country.
Get a job.

Looks me in the eye threateningly. I'm in a bourgeois panic and have no response. I don't say: you're right: I don't have hands like that and hands like that built the country, but those who did build the country have not been given equal share, and the neglect and destruction of the work of people over centuries in Iraq/Mesopot. is just like the govt's neglect and destruction of working people here. He stalks off with girlfriend. Need to learn from this.

Hilarious touch - as we're walking a little about 10 minutes later, pass him going in the other direction - our eyes catch, and he immediately gives me a sign - his hand makes and "L"-like shape, and he bangs it into his forehead repeatedly - I'm completely freaked out and scared that it's some Nazi thing - Doug laughs and tells me it's "Loser."

::

Two young white British women and their silent white male companion - middle classy but Yoof affected - plus a white old-school UFT guy who has glommed onto us and been yelling at people - challenges one of the women as to why she's for the war - she says, "I have my reasons" and the guys says - "What are they??" - she just looks at him - he repeats it, with maniacal glee - she says, "I can't listen to this" - and turns quickly with other woman in tow - sentry looks at us sympathetically - and follows.

::

A white German-looking guy with professional-looking video equipment is filming us, sweeping the crowd of steps and back.

::

An Af-Am guy w/ close cropped hair and wraparounds late 20s early 30s - w/ two friends - he stops to talk and they keep going - specifics of the library and museum sackings - some back and forth over how it could have been prevented - I get to that I didn't know what else to do except make this sign - as he's leaving: "I'm with you, you keep doing your thing."

::

Doug meanwhile in long, friendly but pointed exchange with stocky white male Gulf War vet now TV news cameraman over whether the troops could have prevented plunder - chipping away at his story - but the yelling guy keeps interrupting, escalating.

Seems like debate, but Doug says not really:

"i know why i get angry when rich people go on and on about tax cuts, but what makes the pro war people so angry about people who are against it?"
"it's like being mad at a fan of the losing team in a sporting event... oh, those people are angry too? i never figured out what made the winning fans so angry & mean either.

"probably not the same thing though.

"the WAR people don't act like winners, they act like you are really threatening them..."

::

Greta later posts:

"At the Intersection
stopping traffic, small action in iowa city, two weeks ago:
me holding a sign that says 'us out of iraq'
big m.f. SUV, driver 40-ish white male. he shouts
'bitch' and clips me where i stand, knocking the sign
out of my hands. with his big ass m.f. SUV.
i mean really.
& that's what it looks like here."

High-fashion Latina in mid 30s - "Yes, and? They were going to come and kill us."

::

Realize standing there that "Who Stole..." is a page right out
of Baraka -

Ok - but wld. he see as another theft -

later recall Steve Burt remarking (ironically, since was re: deep image
or something) that when members get proprietary over techniques,
literary movements fall apart - but yet, materialist analysis in a way
yields allusions and steals as stolen labor - art and market capital
share this quality - the knock-off - the sellable parody - the incorpo-
ration - who gets to go home after this?

the sign as pressure valve

::

Sun setting behind museum - different little groups catching last
warm patches - lots of eyes on the sign but no one wants to talk -
lots of fatigue.

::

White woman mid-40s - middle class brown hair loose shortish and a
little frizzy - thick but not overdone lipstick - looking intently, looks
up slow - "The whole time we were in there I was thinking: what if
we came in here and stole everything? How would people here feel
about that?" Pause. "We should do it." Eyes far off imagining it.